GRANDPA WON'T WAKE UP

by
simon max hill & Shannon Wheeler

Written by simon max hill

Drawn by Shannon Wheeler

Colors by Tina Ding

Cover by Shannon Wheeler

Asst. Editor Adam Staffaroni

Design by Stephanie Gonzaga

Ross Richie - Chief Executive Officer
Matt Gagnon - Editor-in-Chief
Adam Fortier - VP-New Business
Wes Harris - VP-Publishing
Lance Kreiter - VP-Licensing & Merchandising
Chip Mosher - Marketing Director
Bryce Carlson - Managing Editor

Ian Brill - Editor
Dafna Pleban - Editor
Shannon Watters - Editor
Eric Harburn - Assistant Editor
Adam Staffaroni - Assistant Editor

Brian Latimer - Lead Graphic Designer
Stephanie Gonzaga - Graphic Designer
Phil Barbaro - Director of Finance
Ivan Salazar - Marketing Manager
Devin Funches - Marketing Assistant

A catalog record of this book is available from OCLC and from the BOOM! Studios website, www.boom-studios.com, on the Librarians Page.

BOOM! Studios, 6310 San Vicente Boulevard, Suite 107, Los Angeles, CA 90048-5457. Printed in USA. First Printing. ISBN: 978-1-60886-092-0

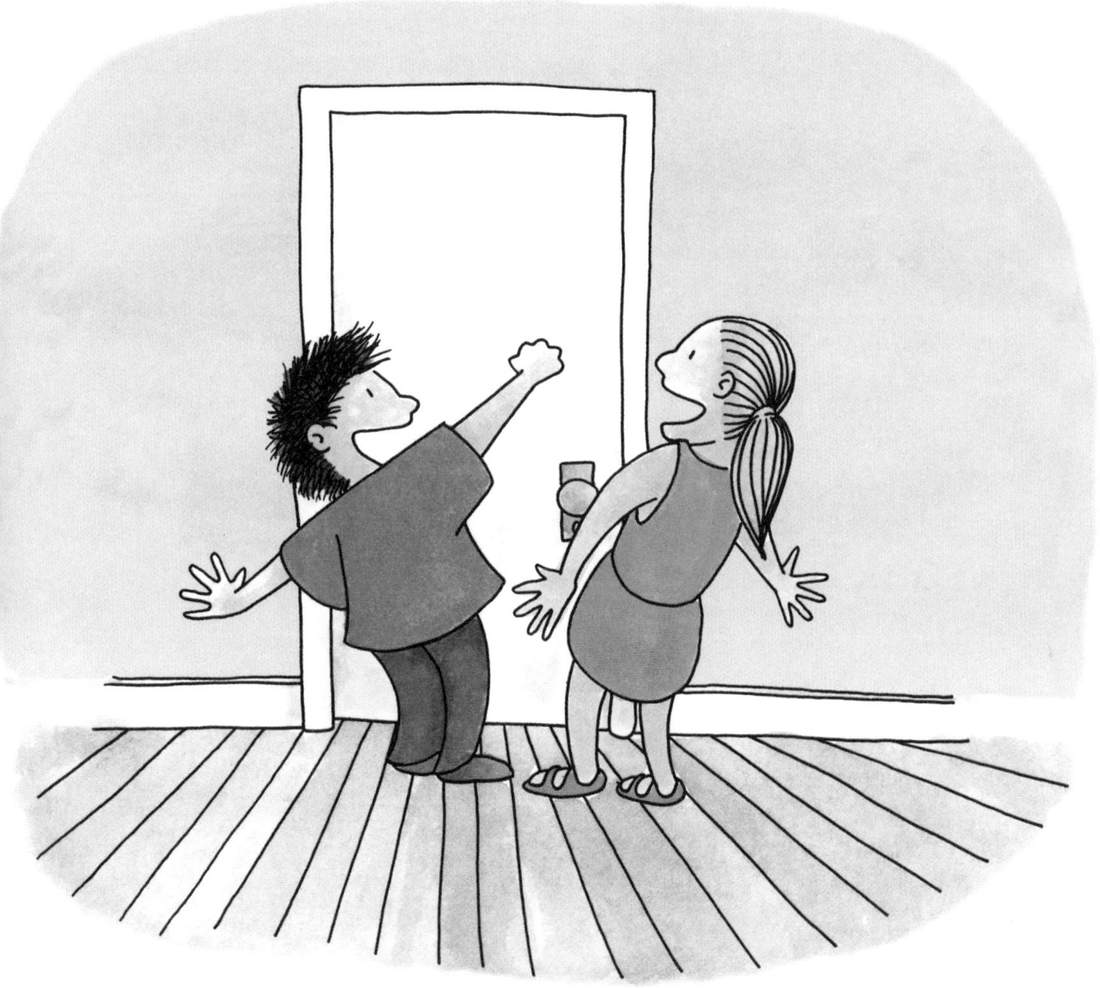

We knocked on Grandpa's door and said,
"Hey Gramps, it's almost noon."

"You said you'd take us to the park,
you said you'd take us soon."

But Grandpa didn't answer us,
sometimes he's such a creep.

And when we burst into his room
Grandpa was still asleep!

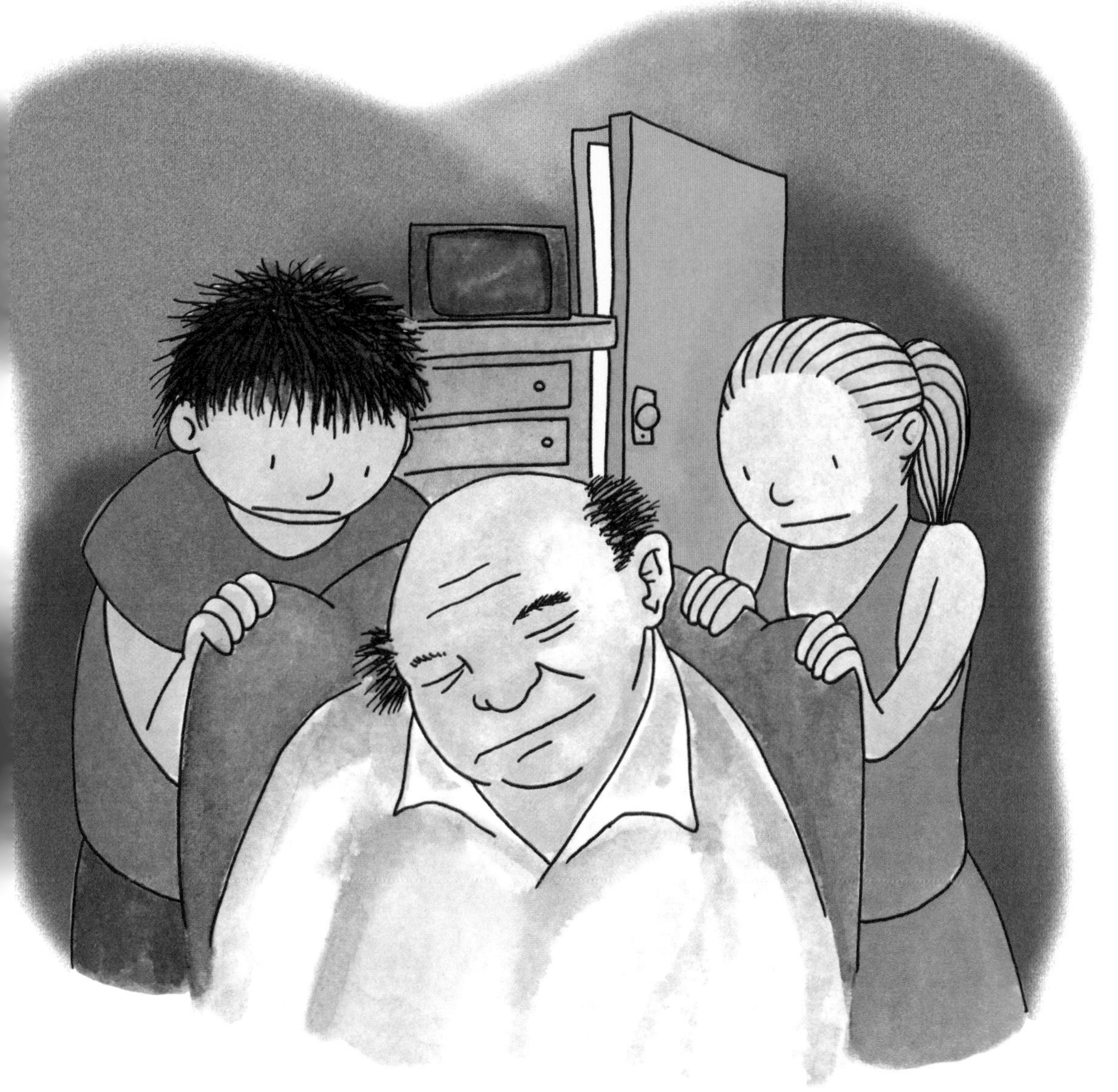

So we turned on the Tee Vee,

but Grandpa won't wake up.

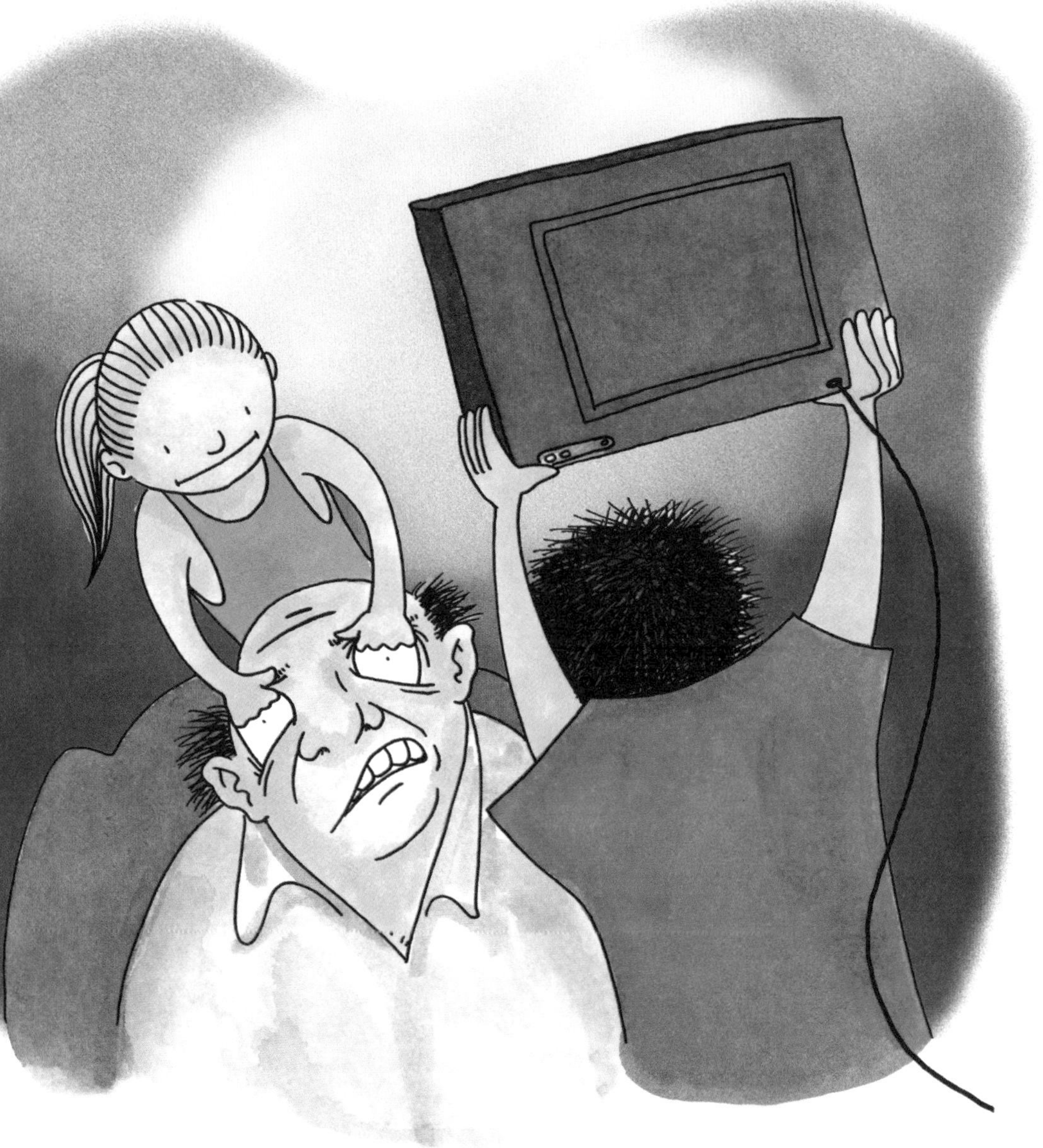

We wondered if he had to pee,

but Grandpa won't wake up.

I clanged a cymbal by his head,

but Grandpa won't wake up.

We pinched his cheeks 'til they turned red,

but Grandpa won't wake up.

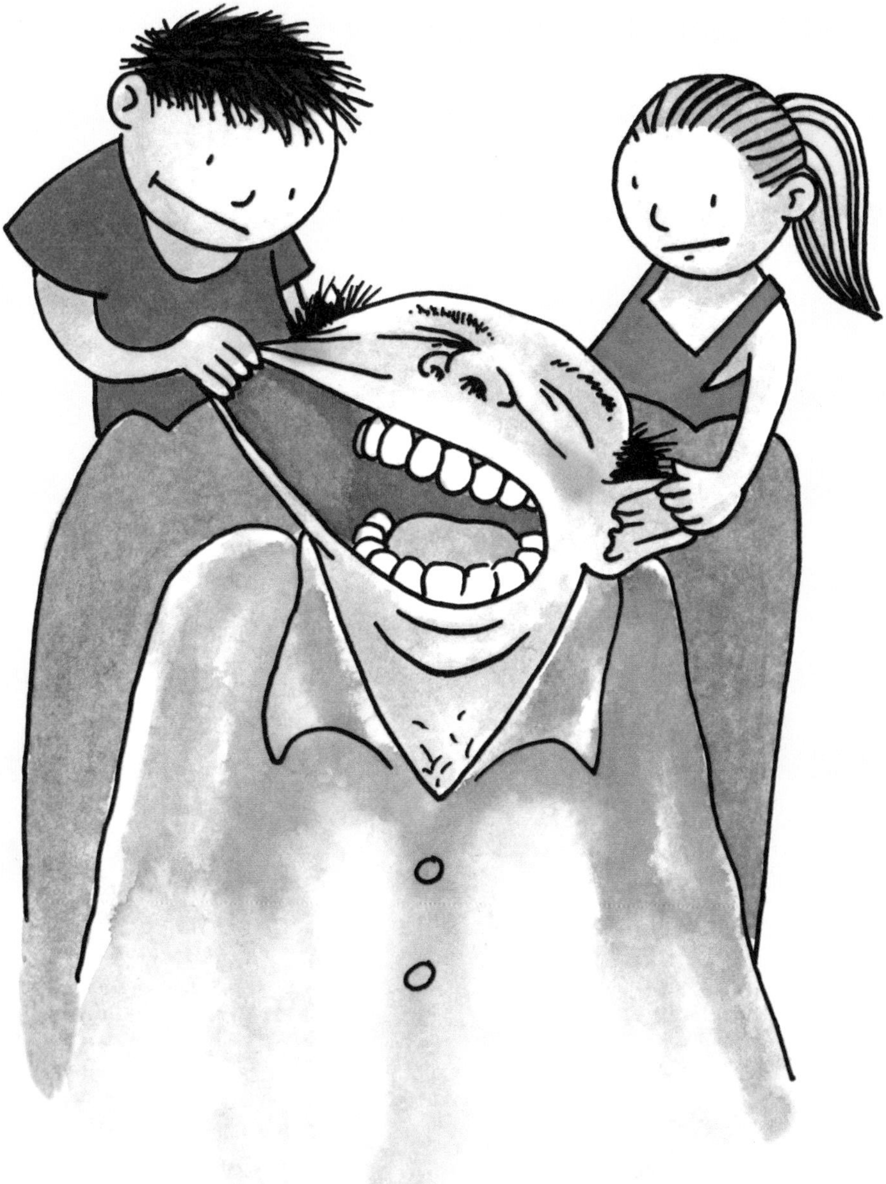

Our Uncle Fred
screamed really loud,

but Grandpa
won't wake up.

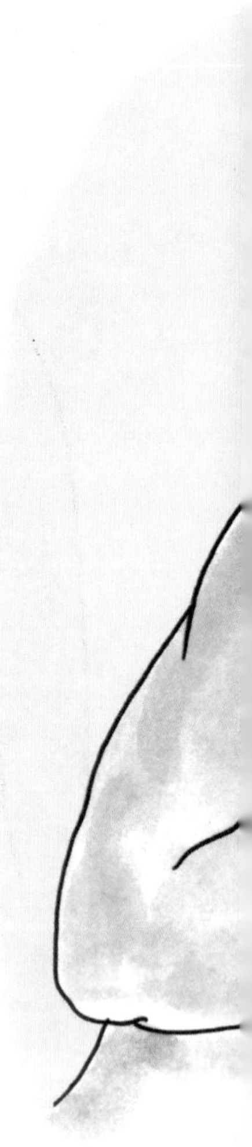

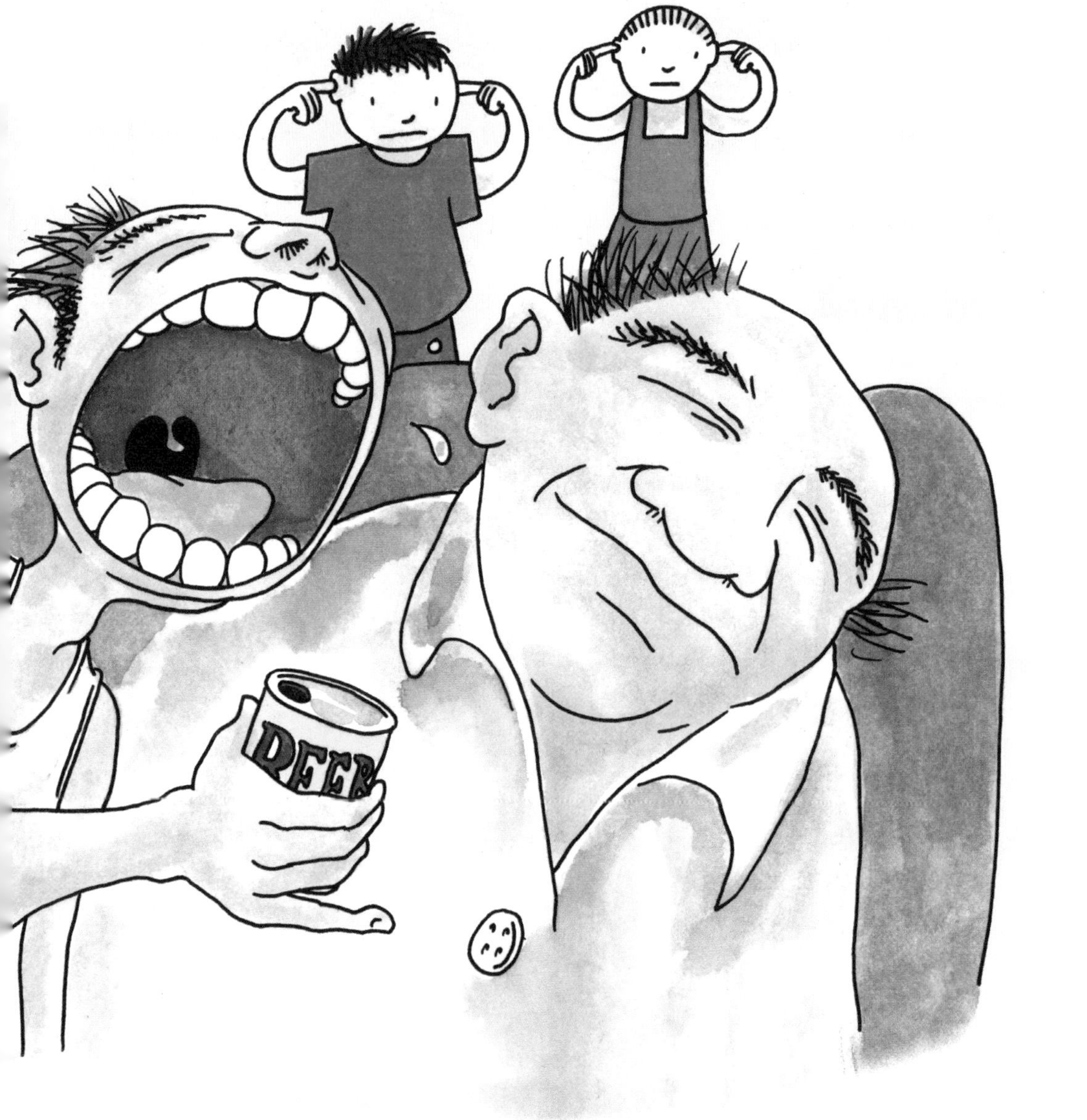
BEER

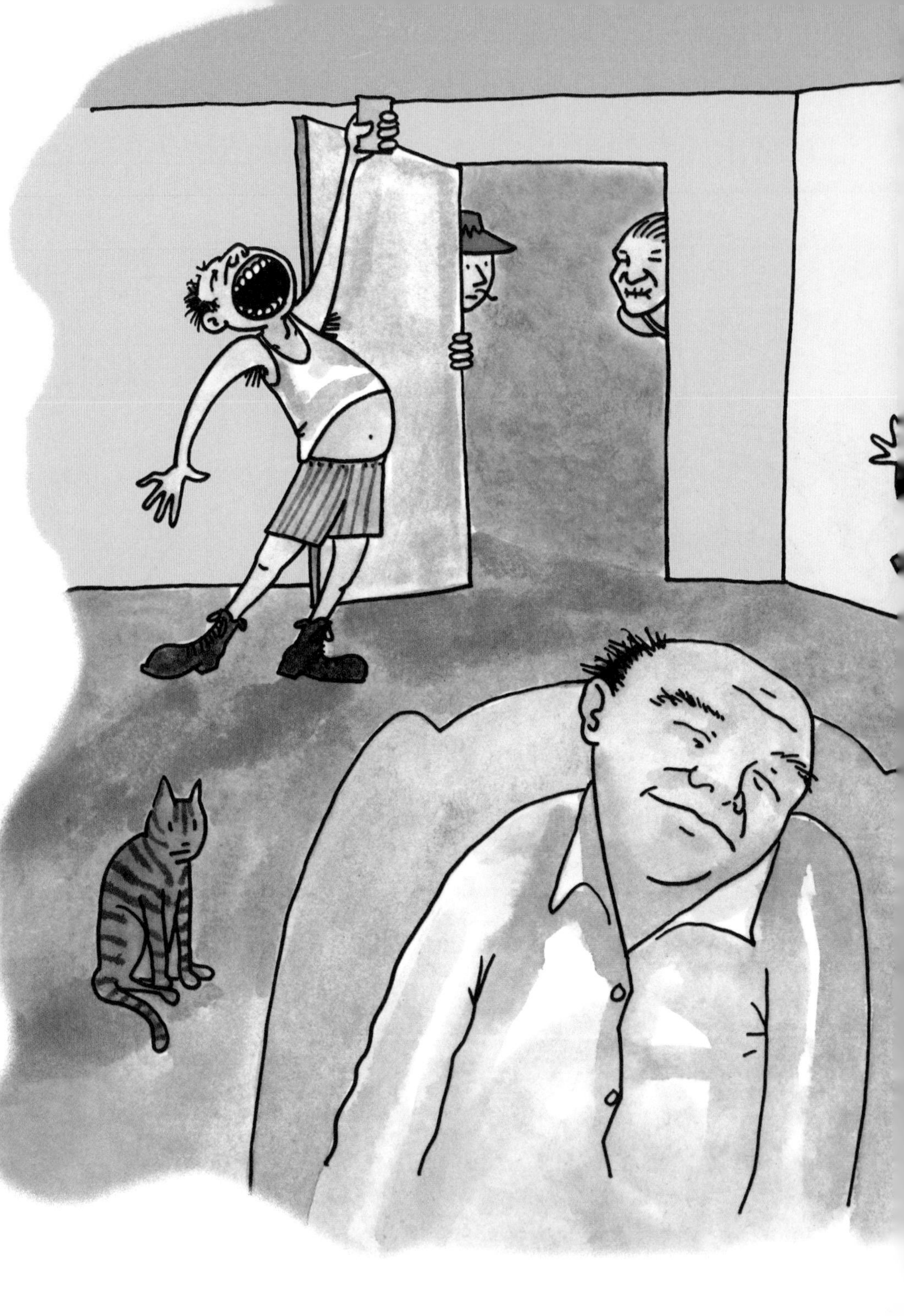

The screaming brought in quite a crowd,

but Grandpa won't wake up.

We painted all his toenails green,

but Grandpa won't wake up.

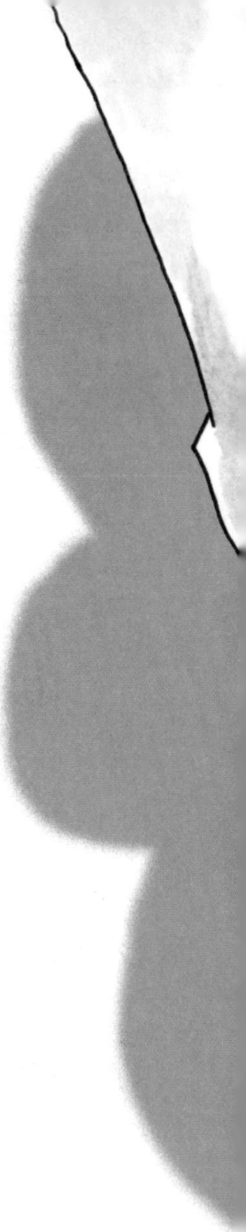

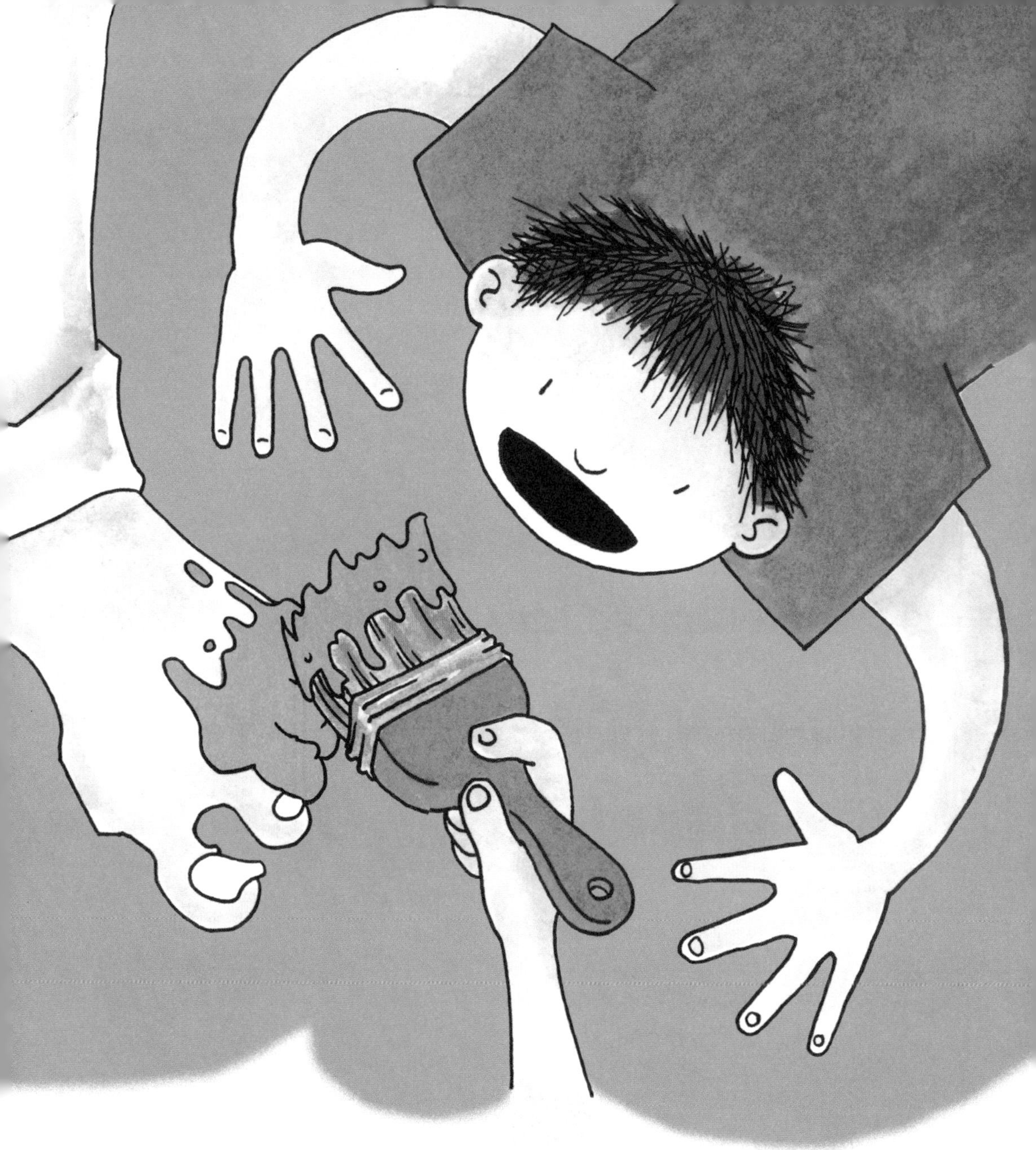

And bounced him on a trampoline,

but Grandpa won't wake up.

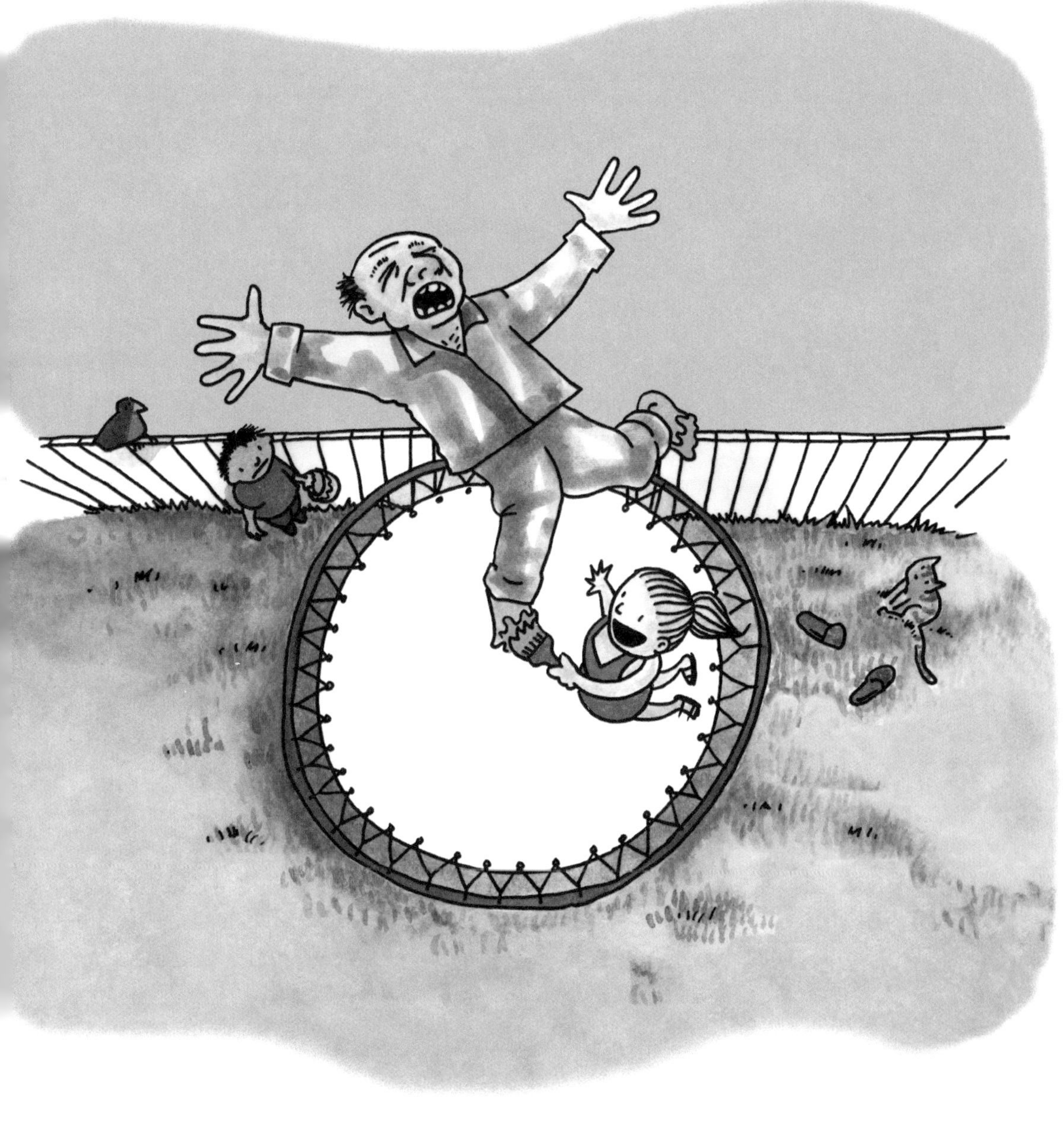

We laid him naked on the lawn,

but Grandpa won't wake up.

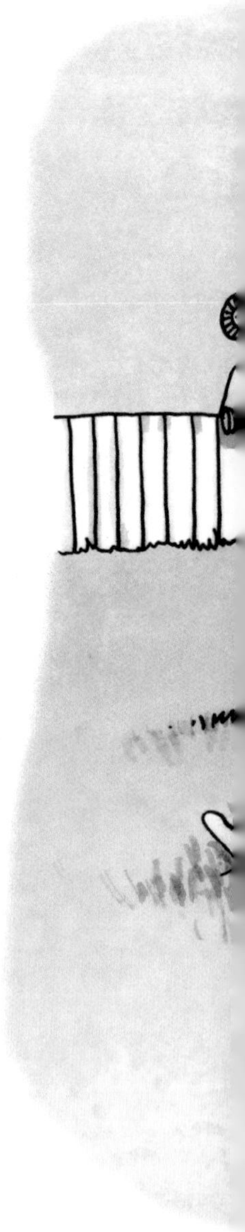

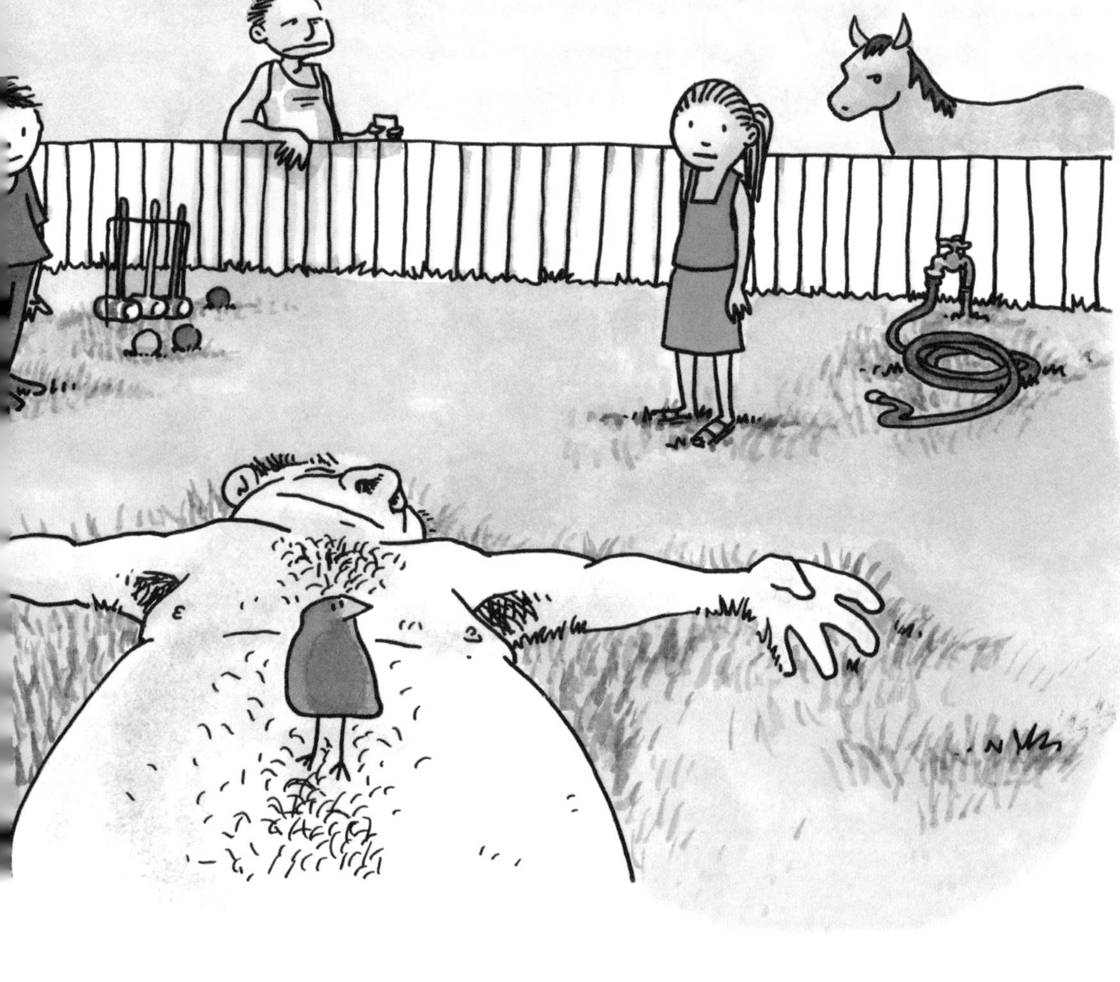

And then we turned the sprinklers on,

but Grandpa won't wake up.

We dressed him up in Nazi clothes,

but Grandpa won't wake up.

And added fishnet pantyhose,

but Grandpa won't wake up.

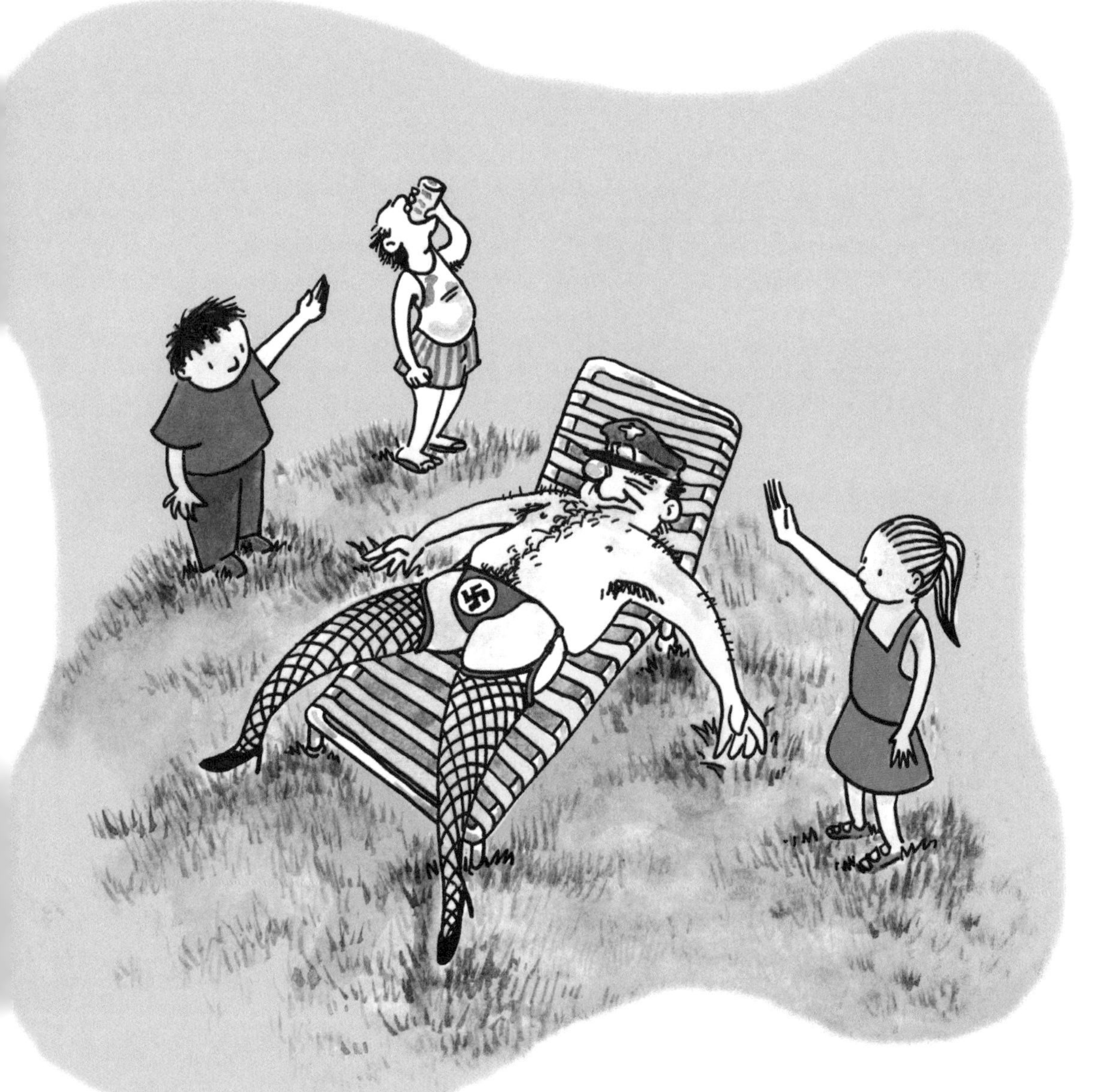

We put warm honey in his pants,

but Grandpa won't wake up.

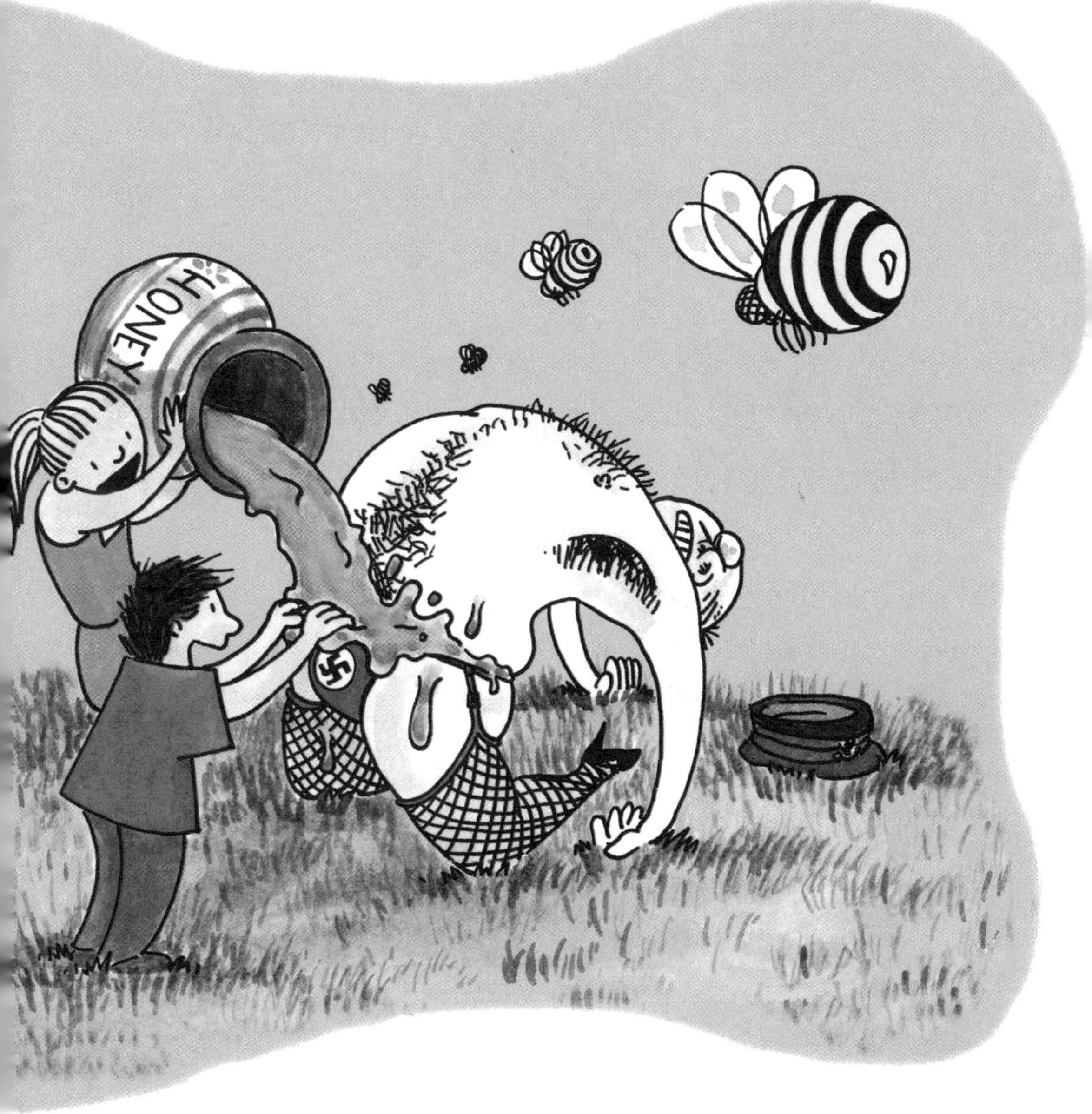
HONEY

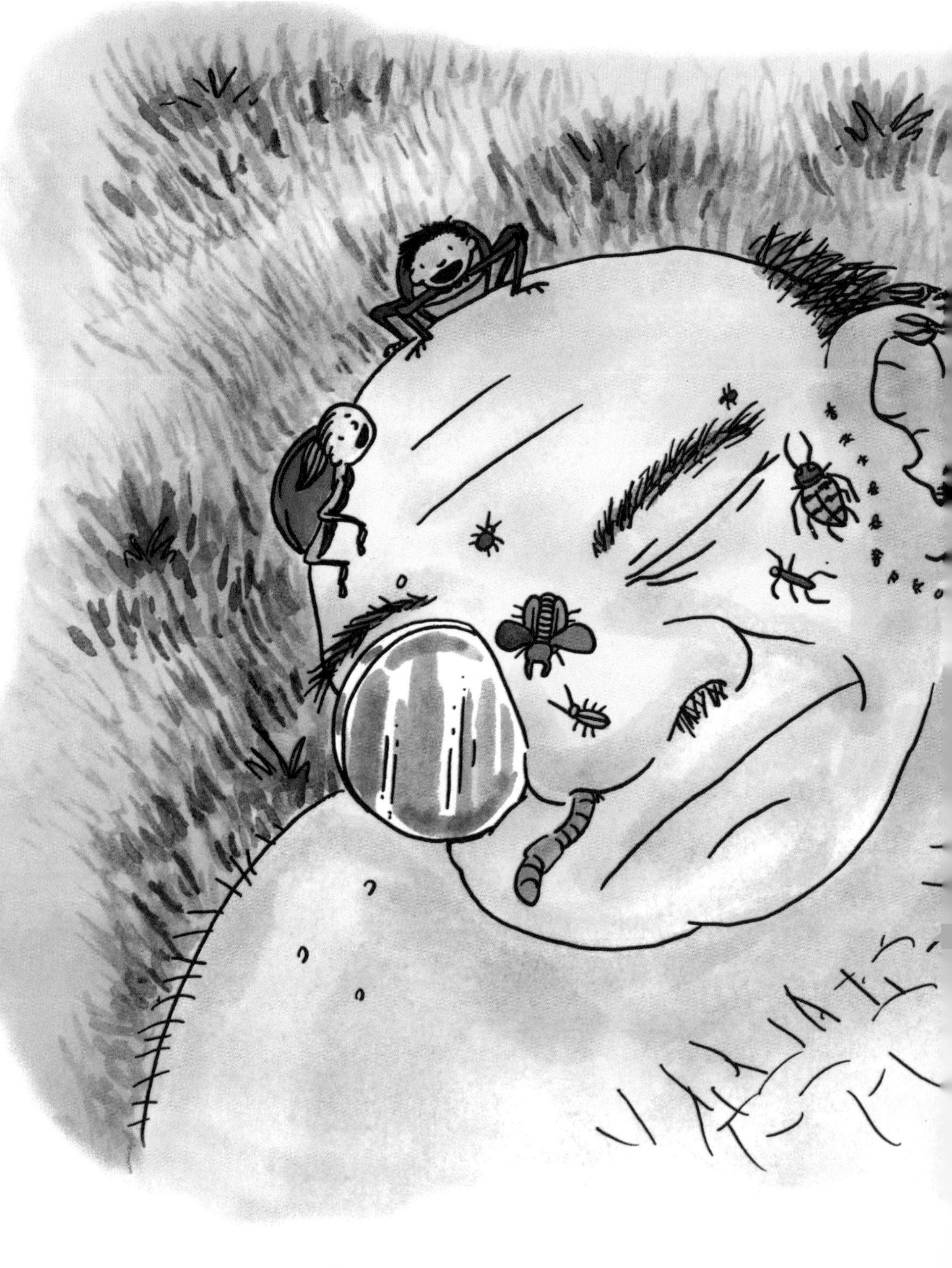

And covered him with
bugs and ants,

but Grandpa won't
wake up.

For weeks we kept him in a tree,

but Grandpa won't wake up.

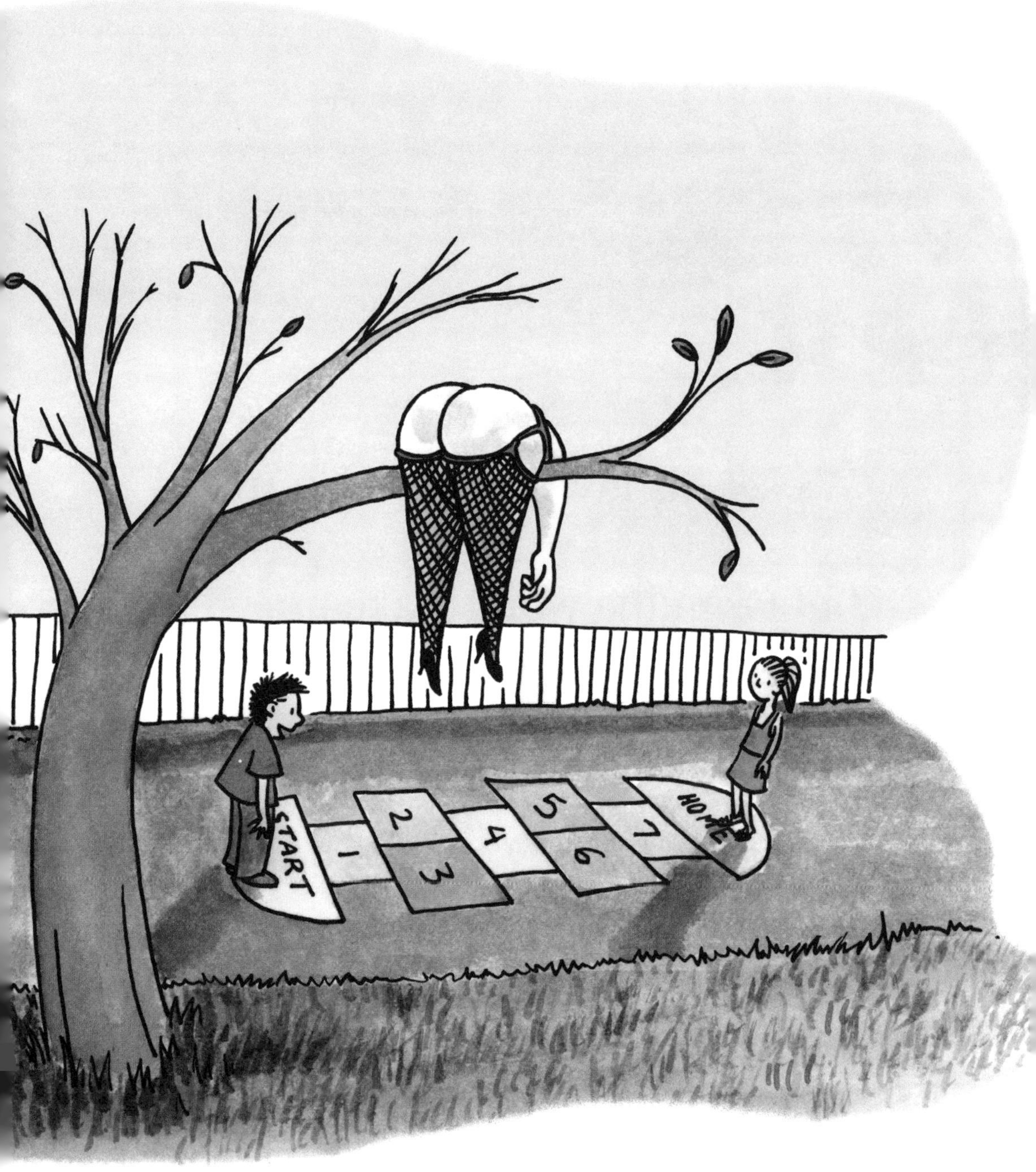
START
1
2
3
4
5
6
7
HOME

We set his favorite goldfish free,

but Grandpa won't wake up.

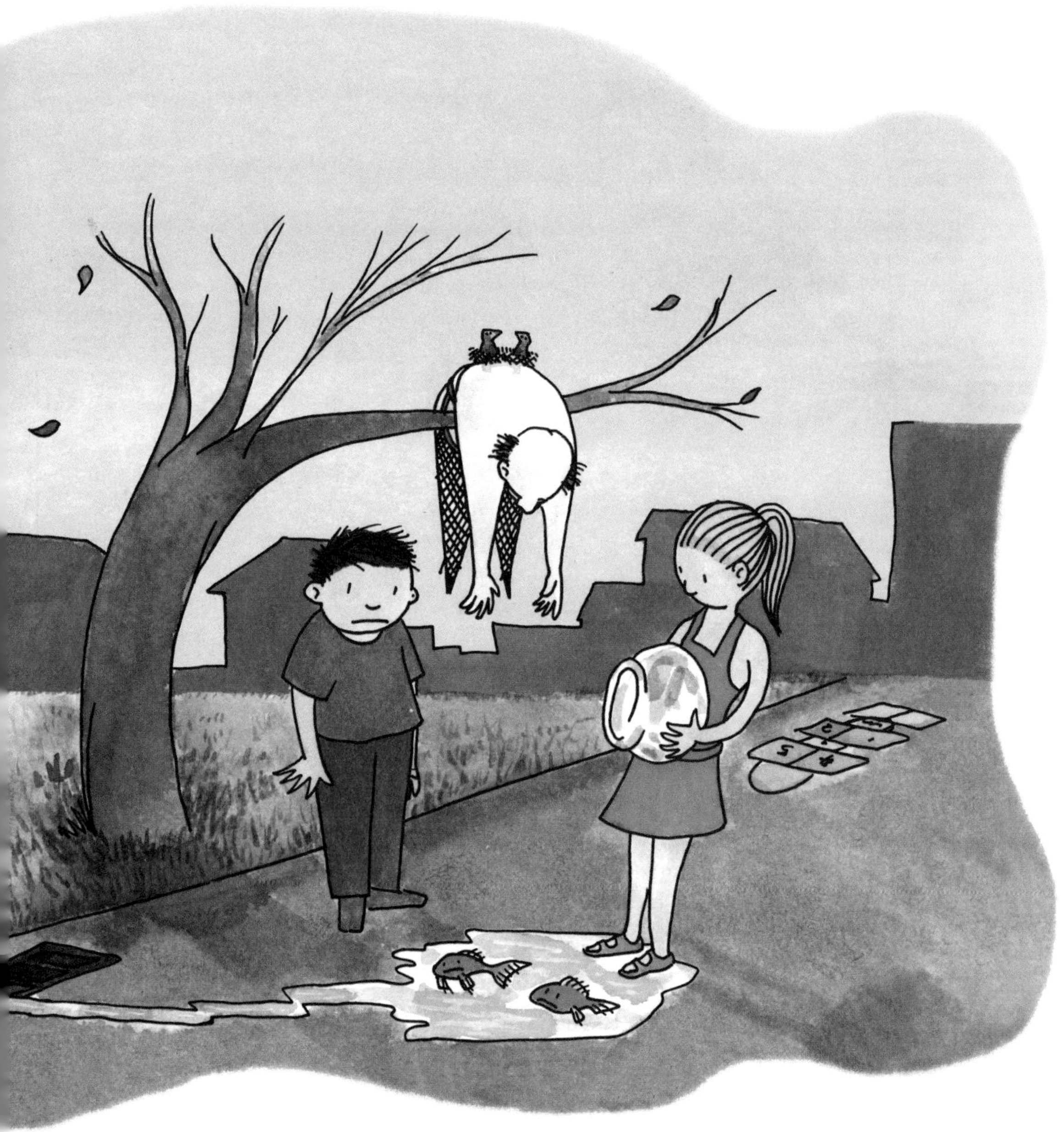

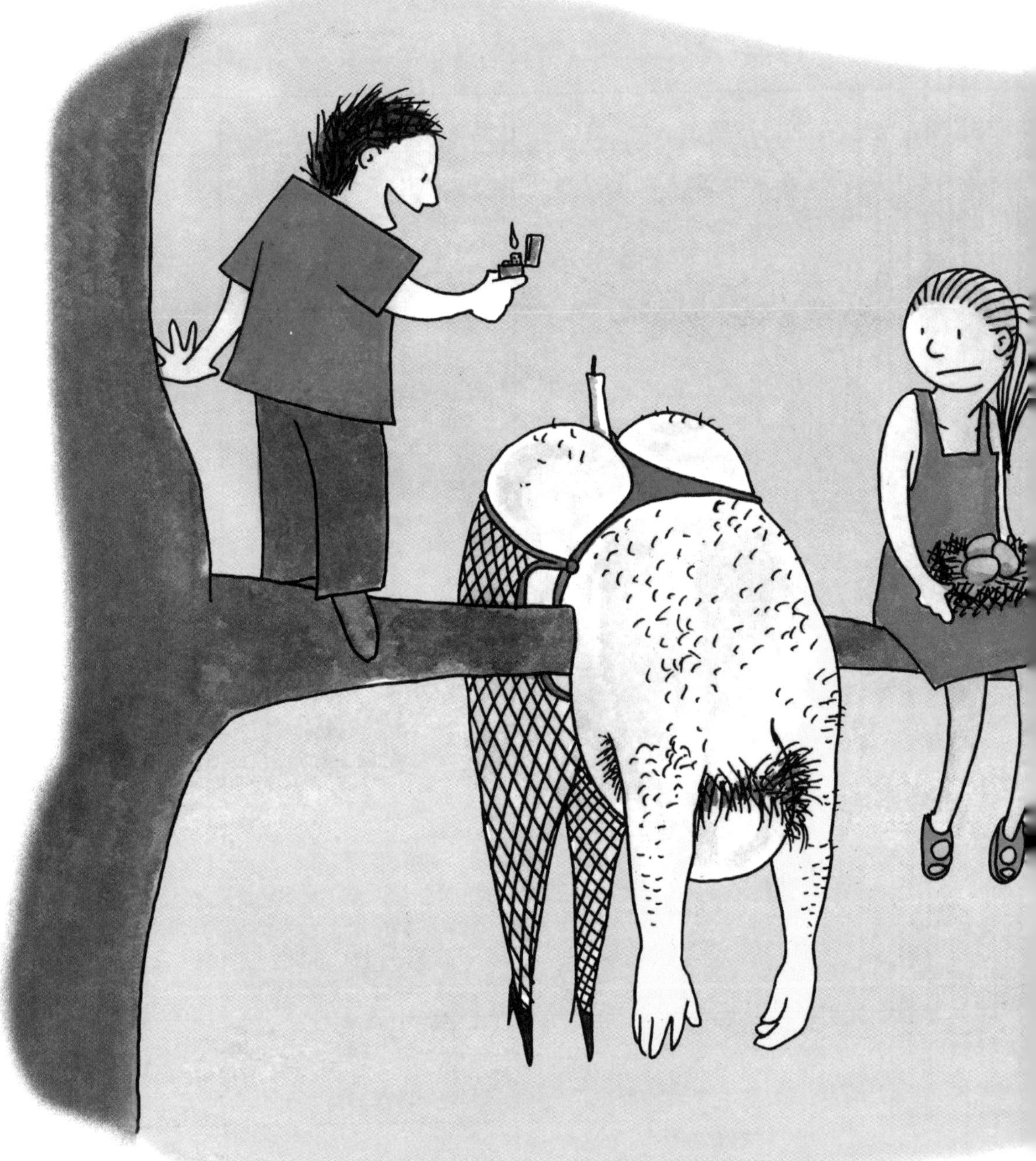

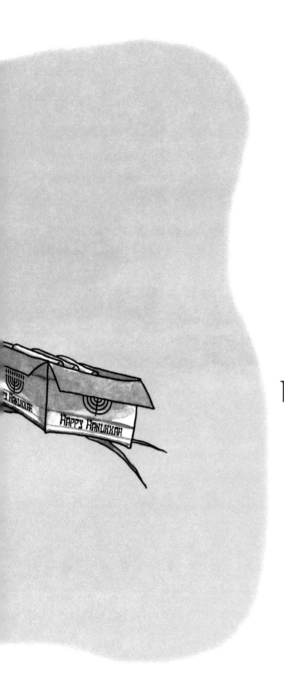

We lit a candle in
his butt,

but Grandpa won't
wake up.

Grandma punched him in the nuts,

but Grandpa won't wake up.

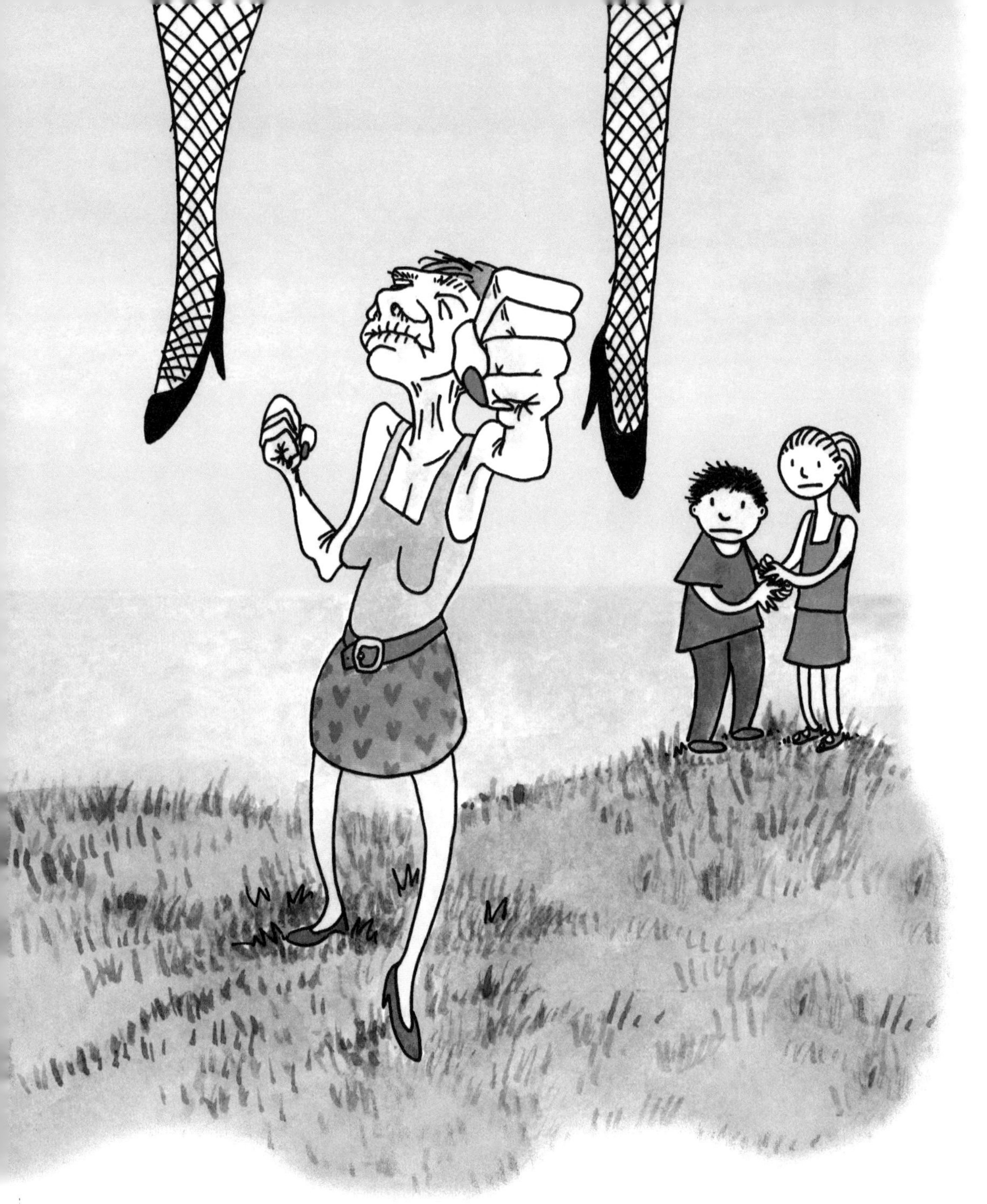

We beat him with
a baseball bat,

but Grandpa
won't wake up.

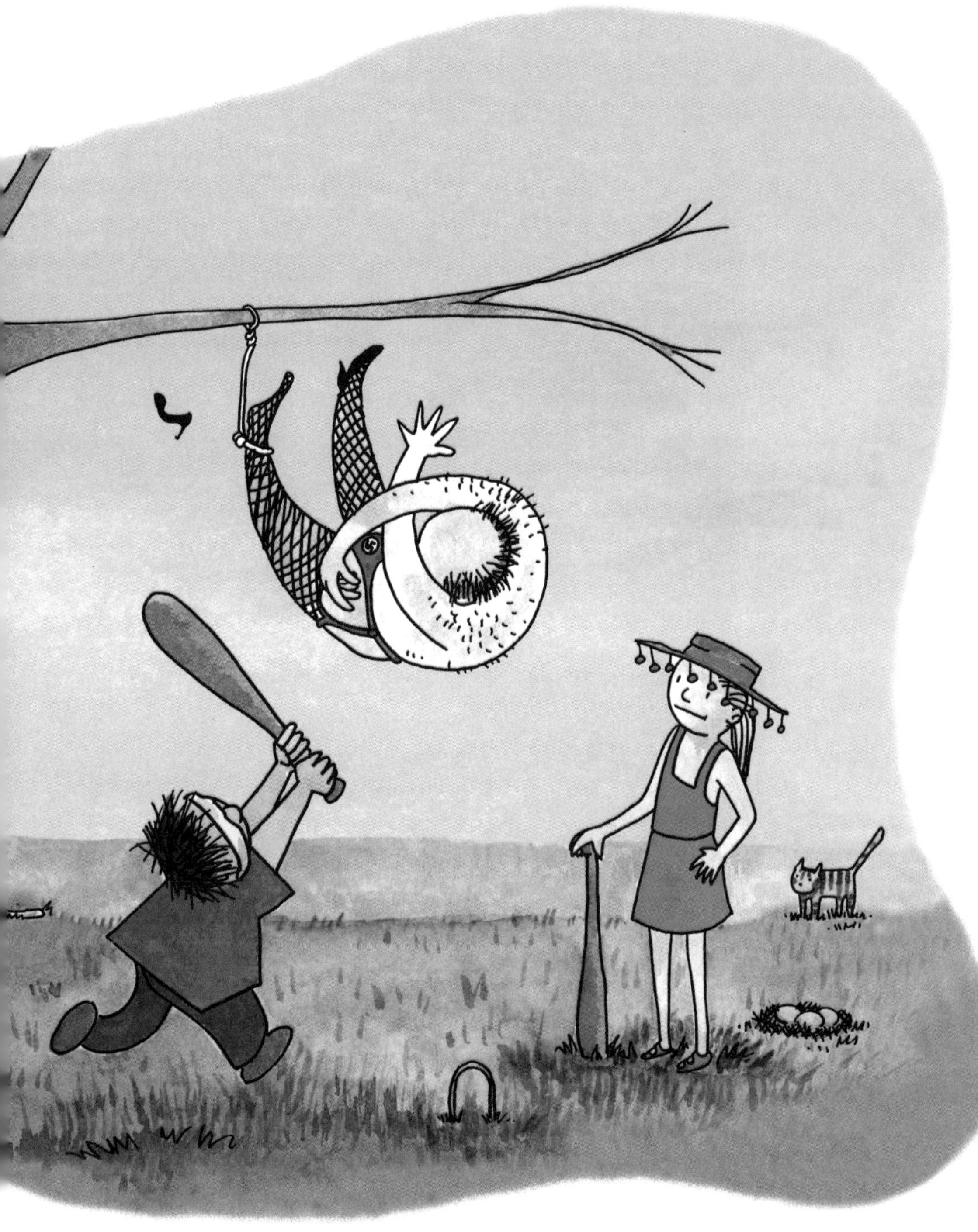

And tied him to an angry cat,

but Grandpa won't wake up.

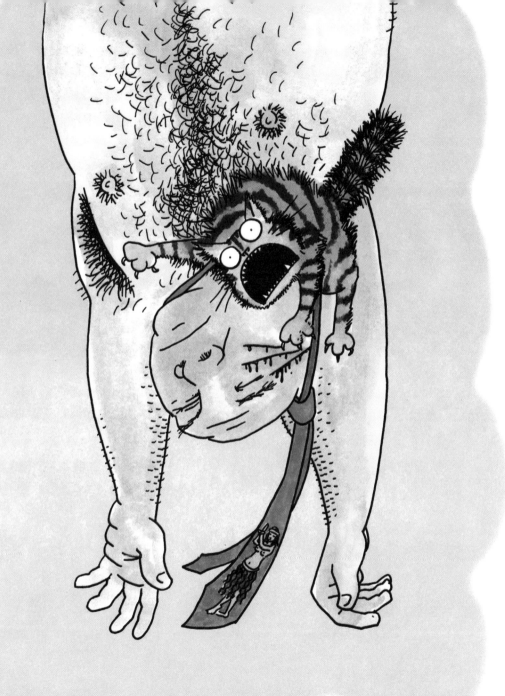

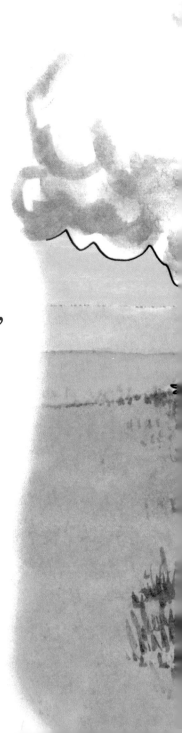

My brother lit his hair on fire,

but Grandpa won't wake up.

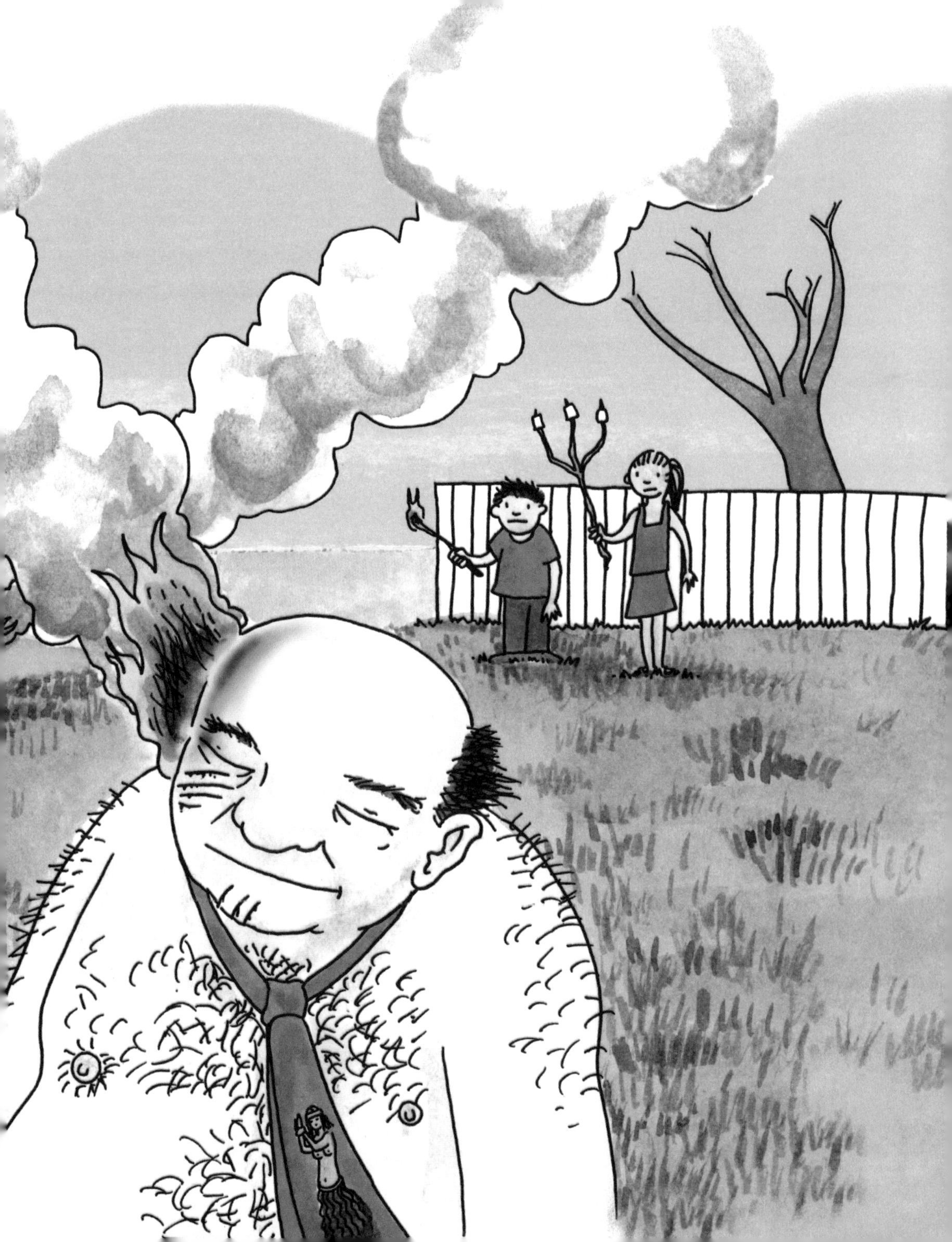

And rolled him in
a tractor tire,

but Grandpa
won't wake up.

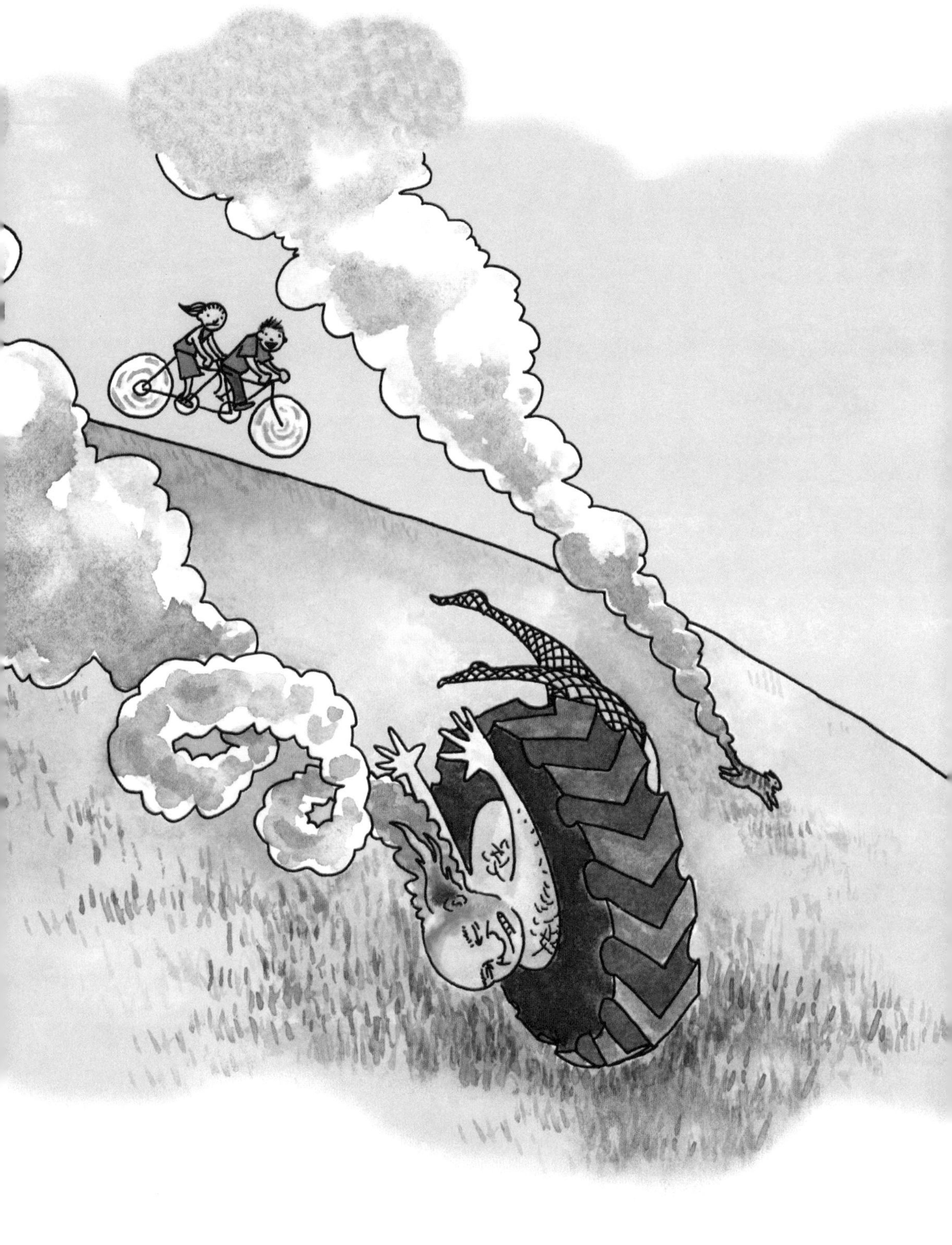

We dropped him from a speeding plane,

but Grandpa won't wake up.

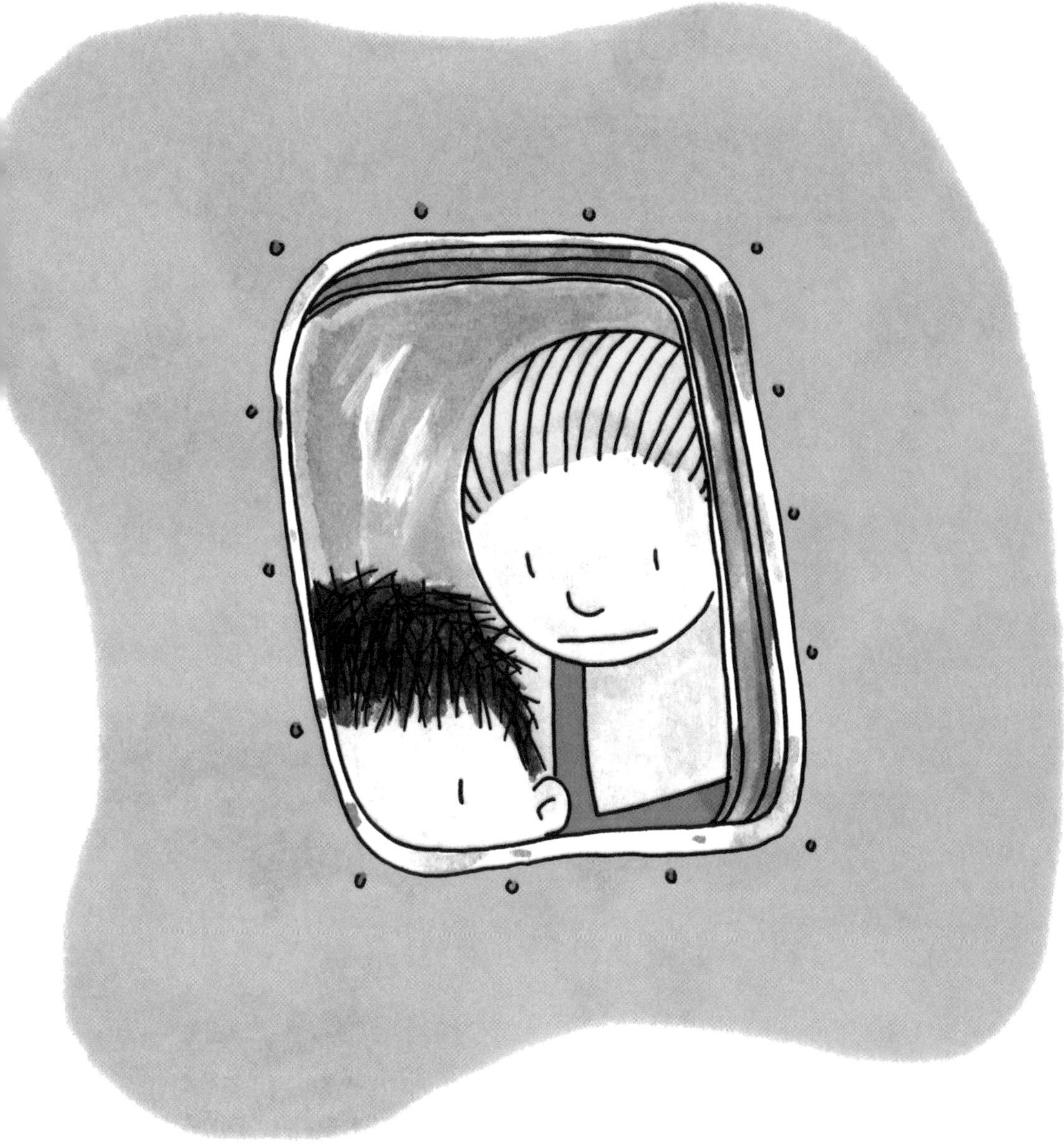

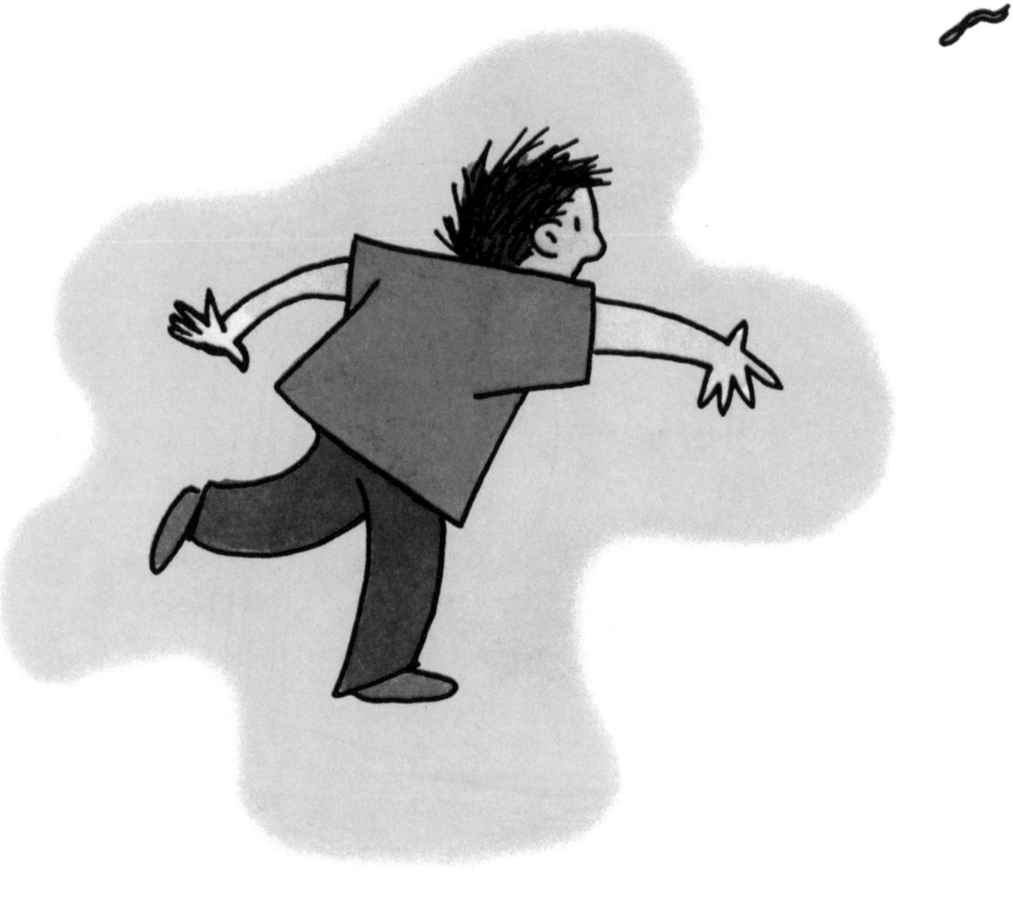

A doctor cut out half his brain,

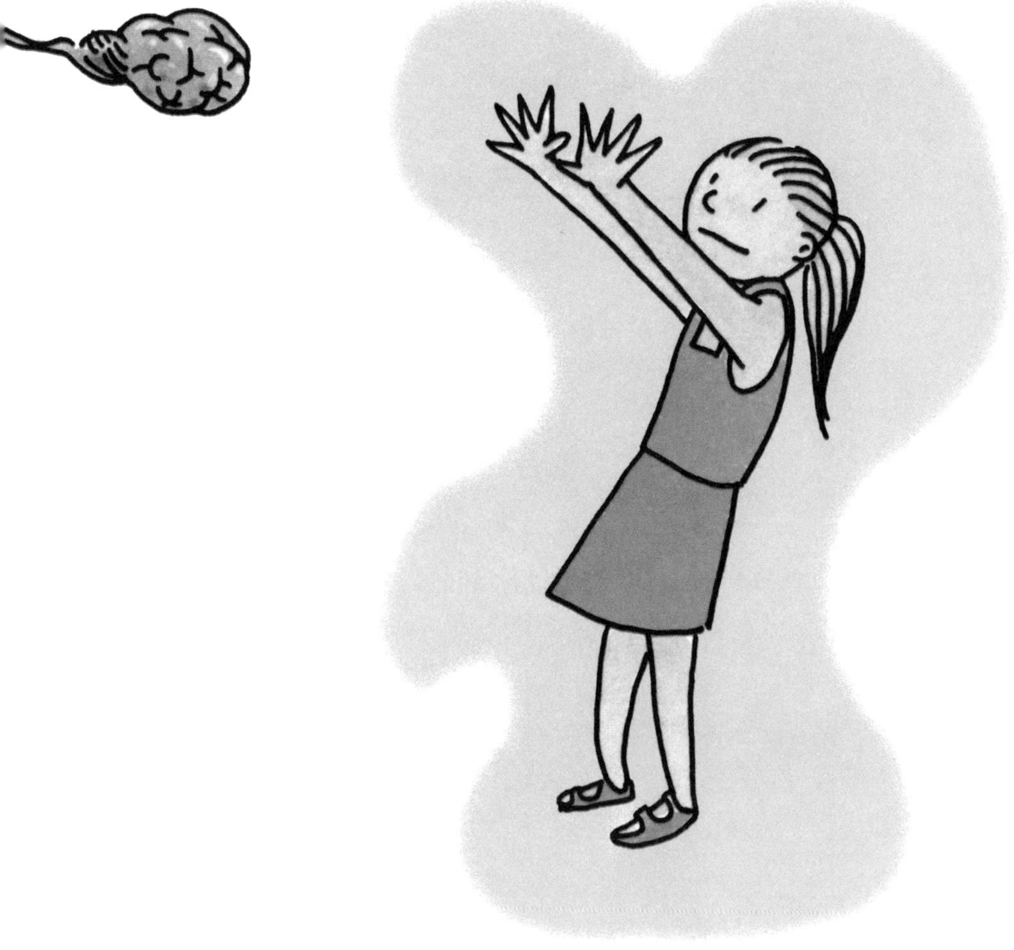

but Grandpa won't wake up.

C'Thris'Klpotheup,

an Elder God that heard our call.

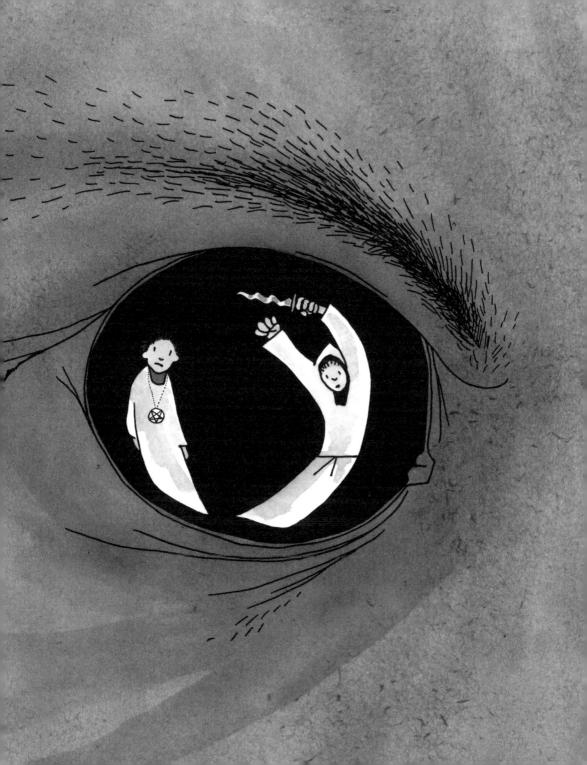

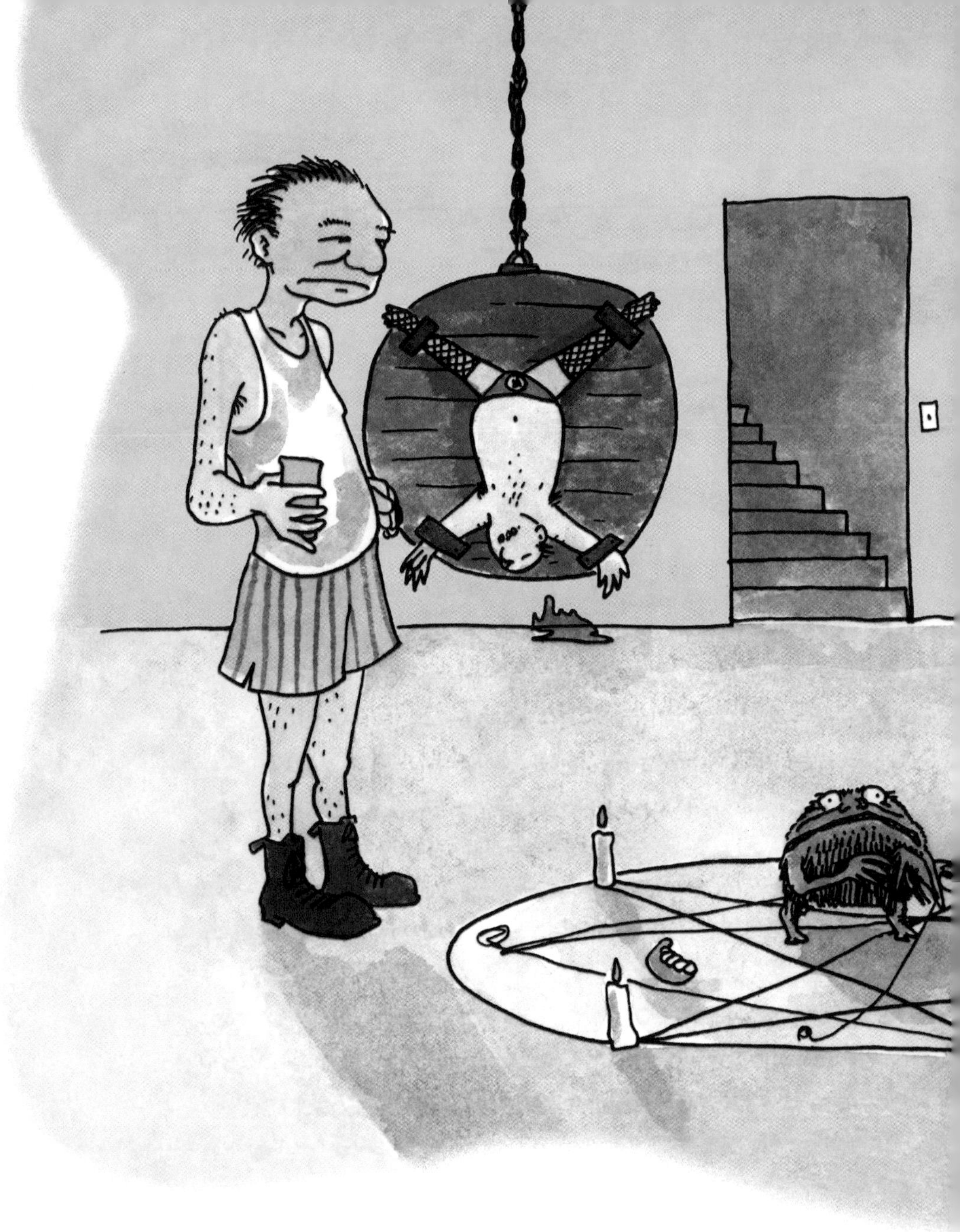

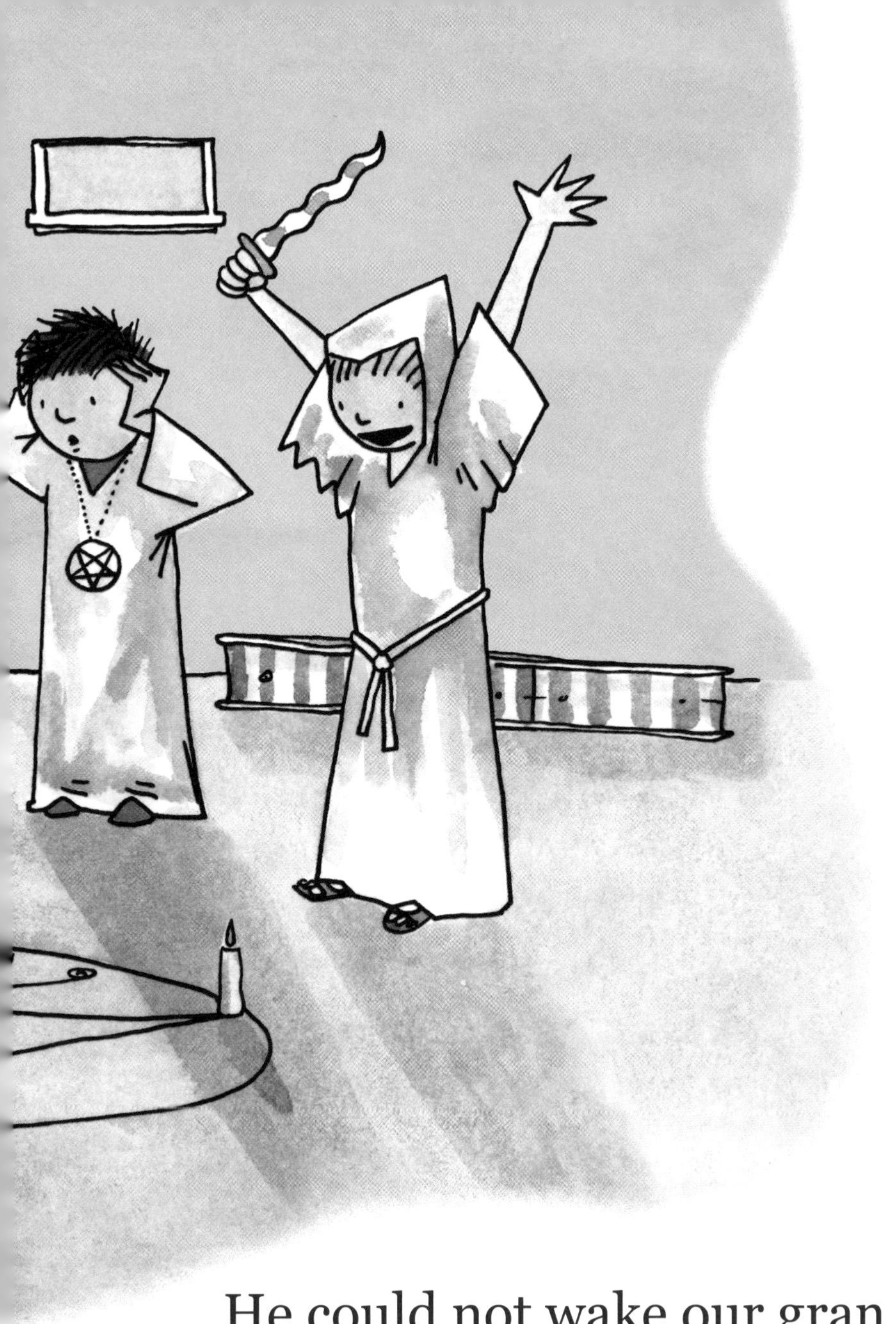

He could not wake our grandpa up,

he's only two feet tall!

We tried everything...

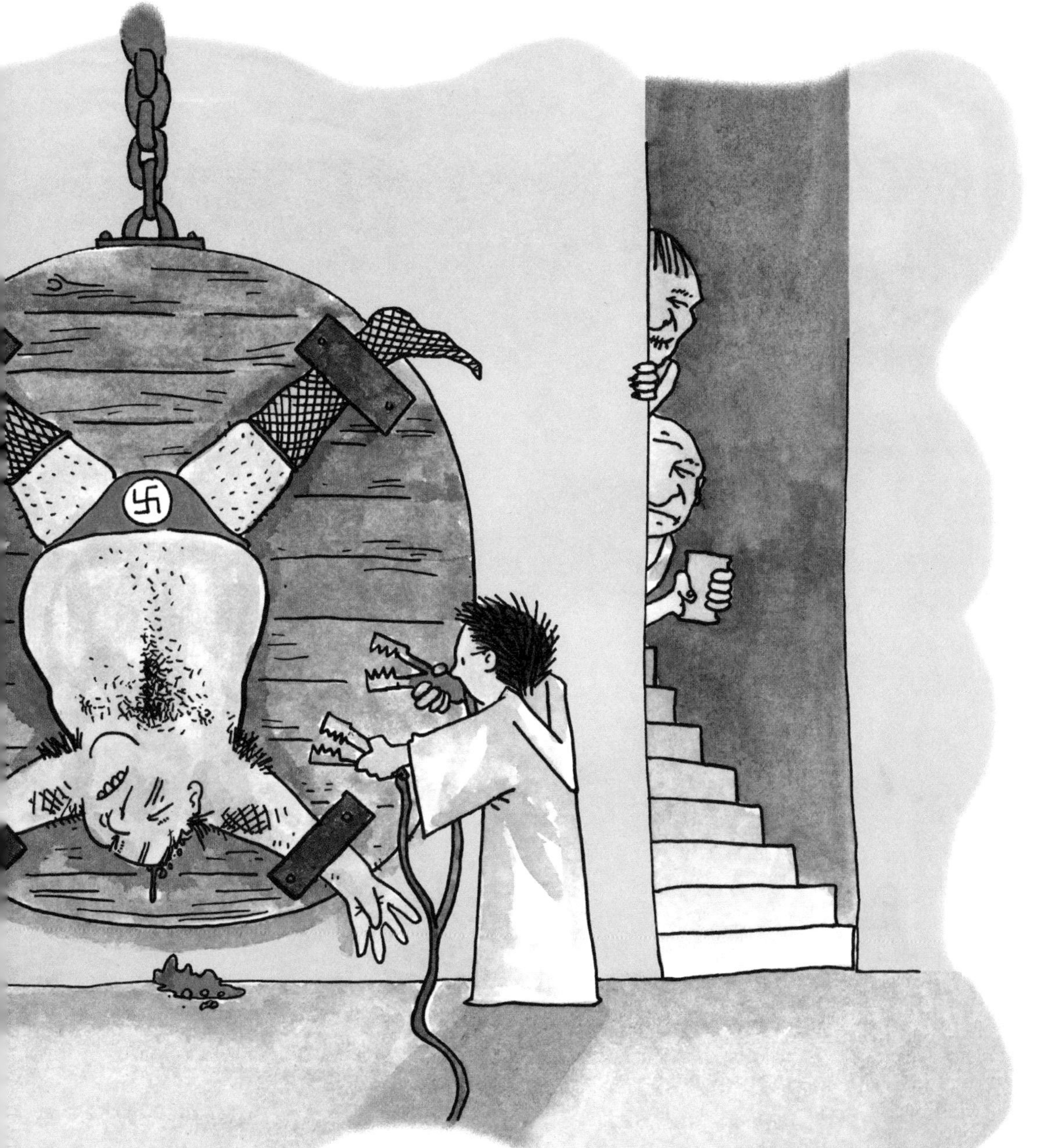

Everything...

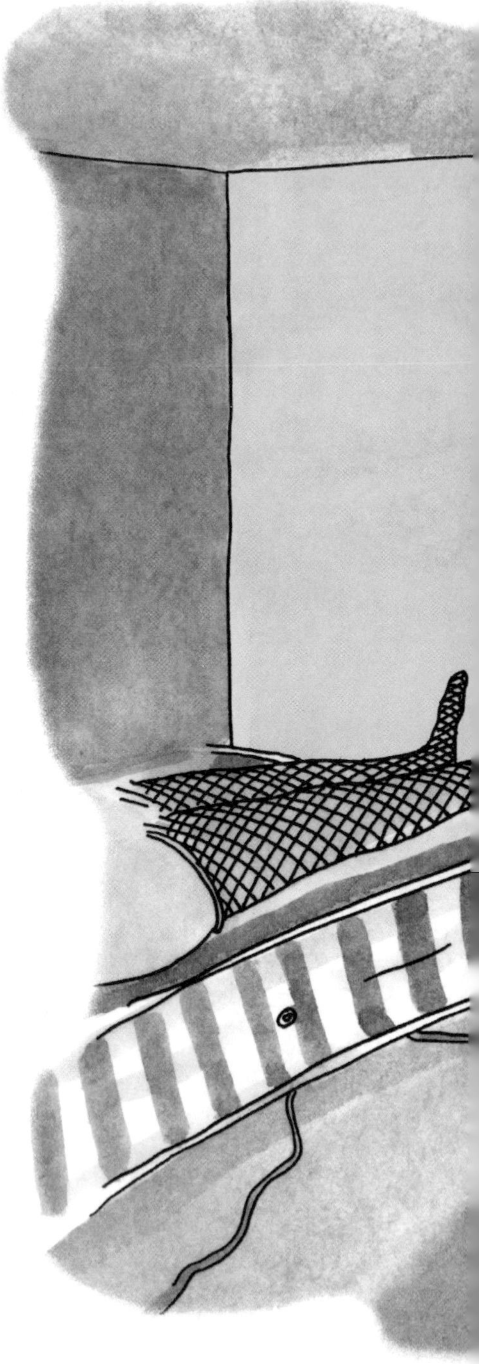

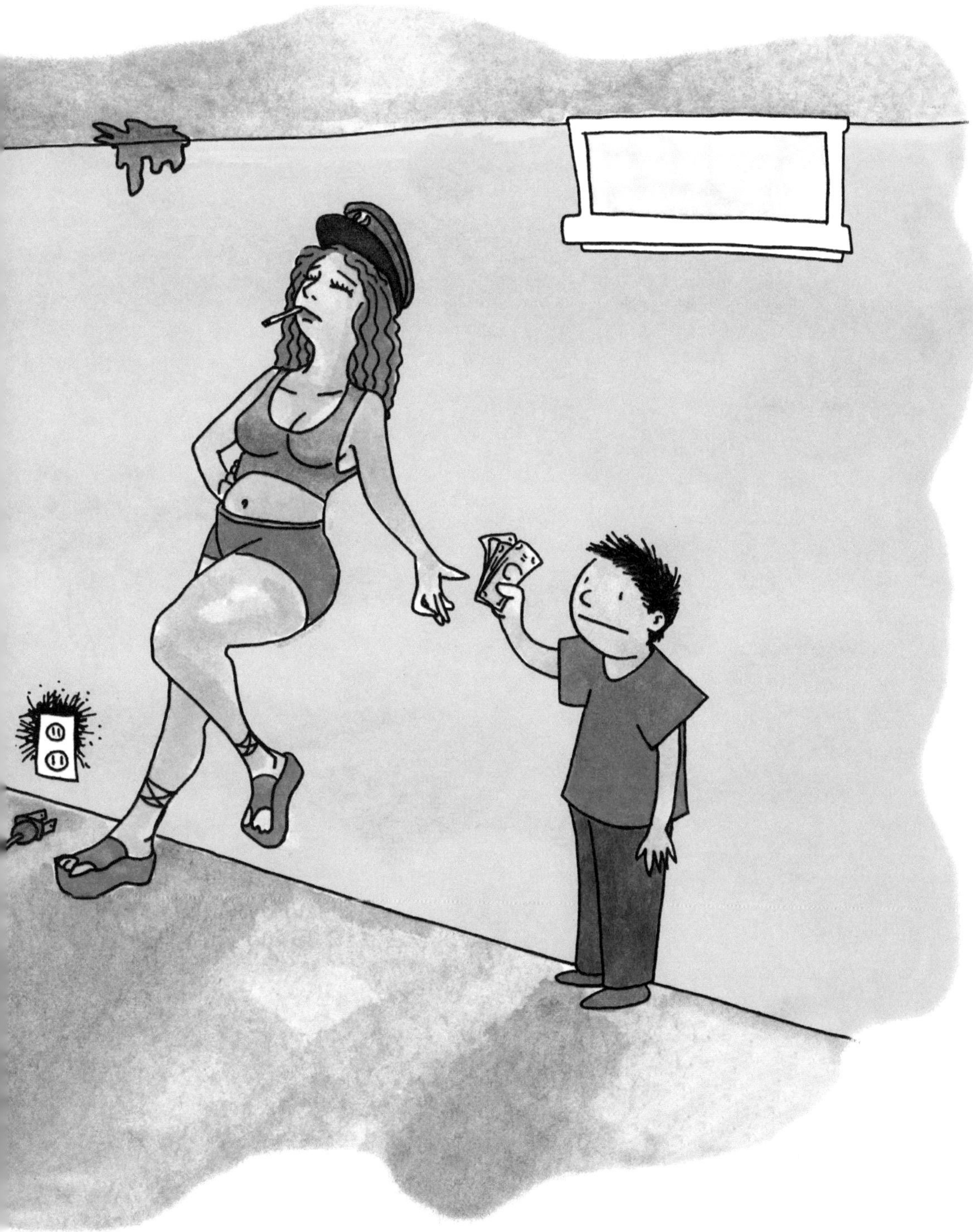

Everything...

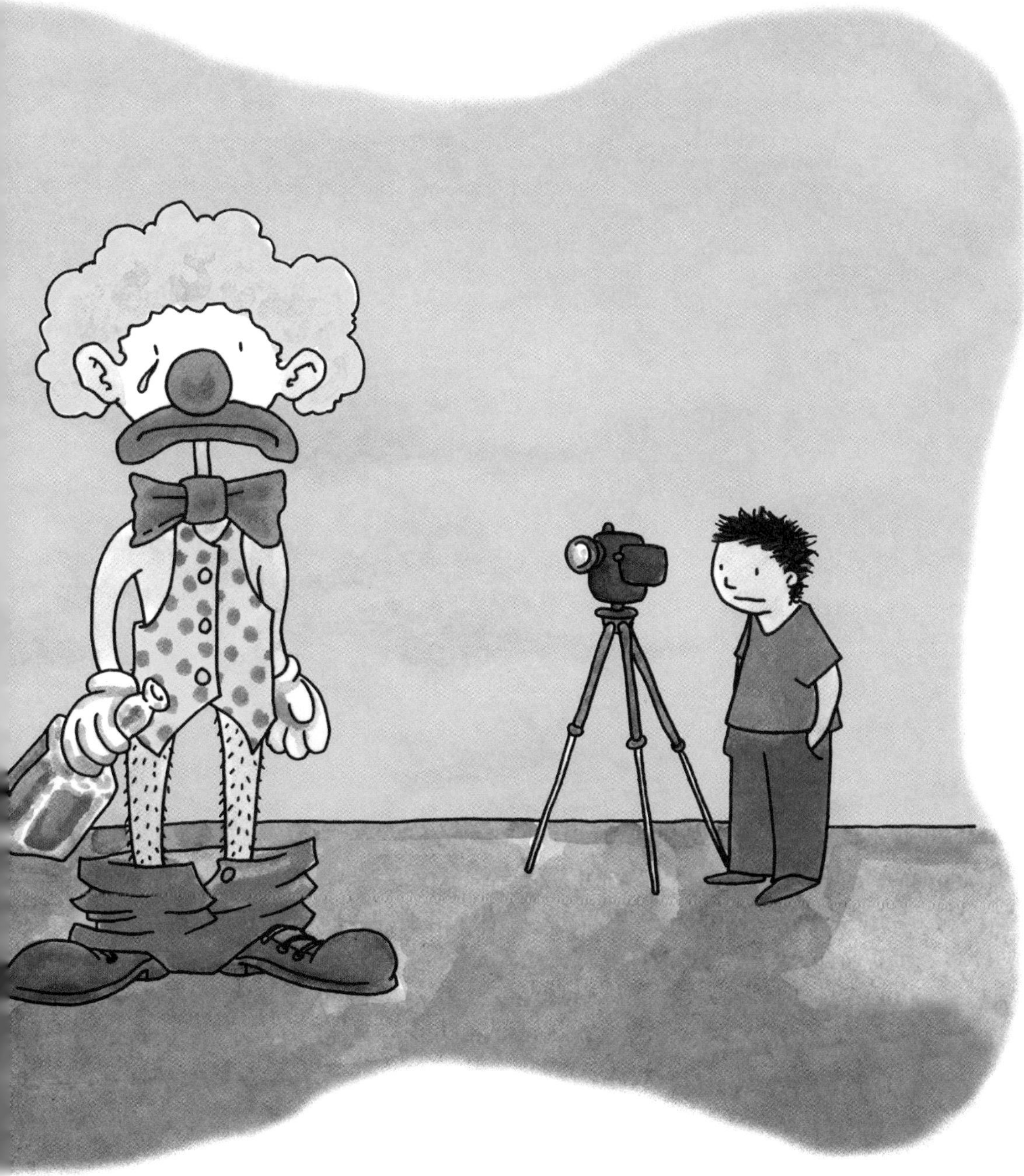

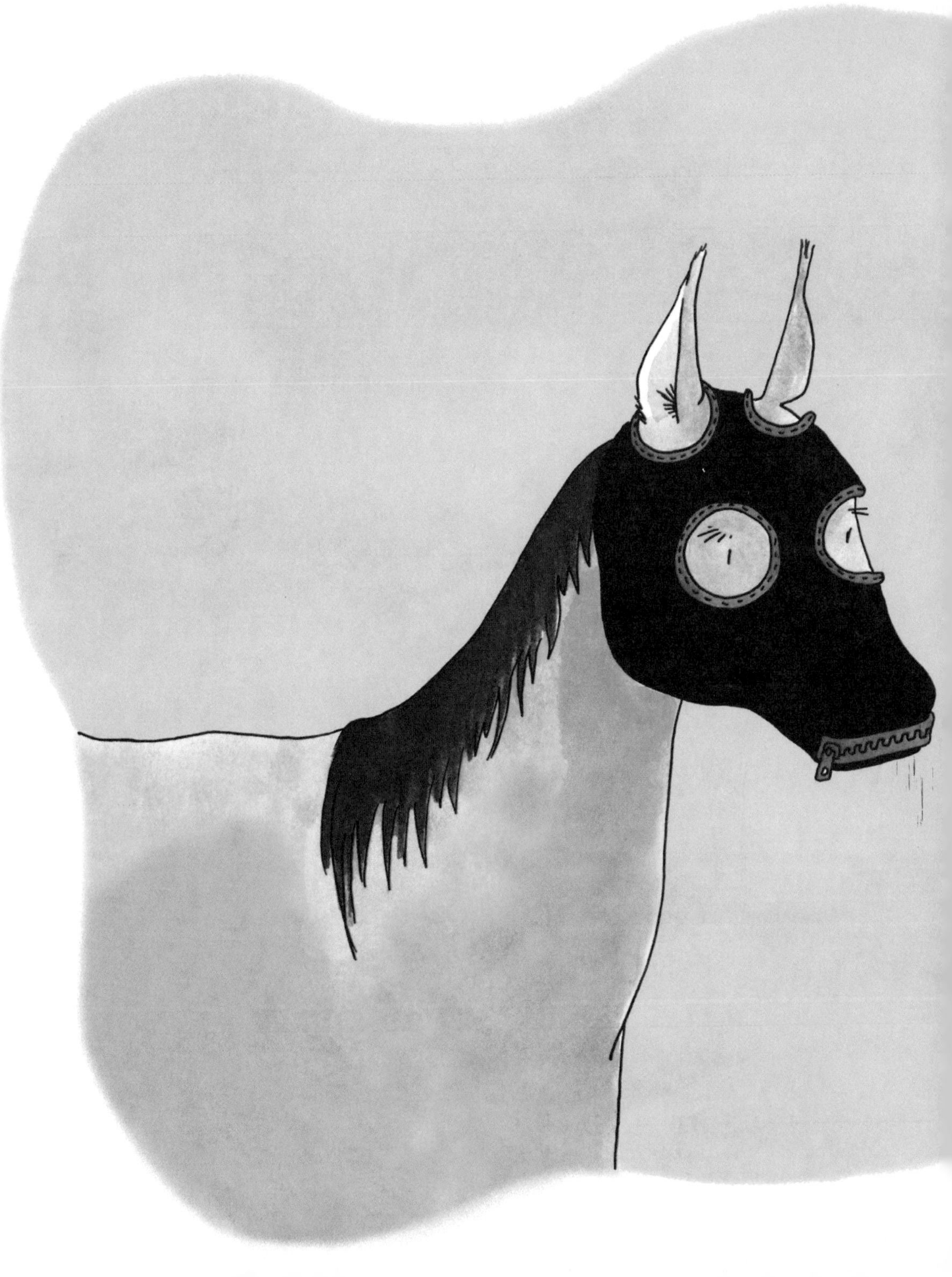

EVERYTHING...

Everything I could imagine in my head...

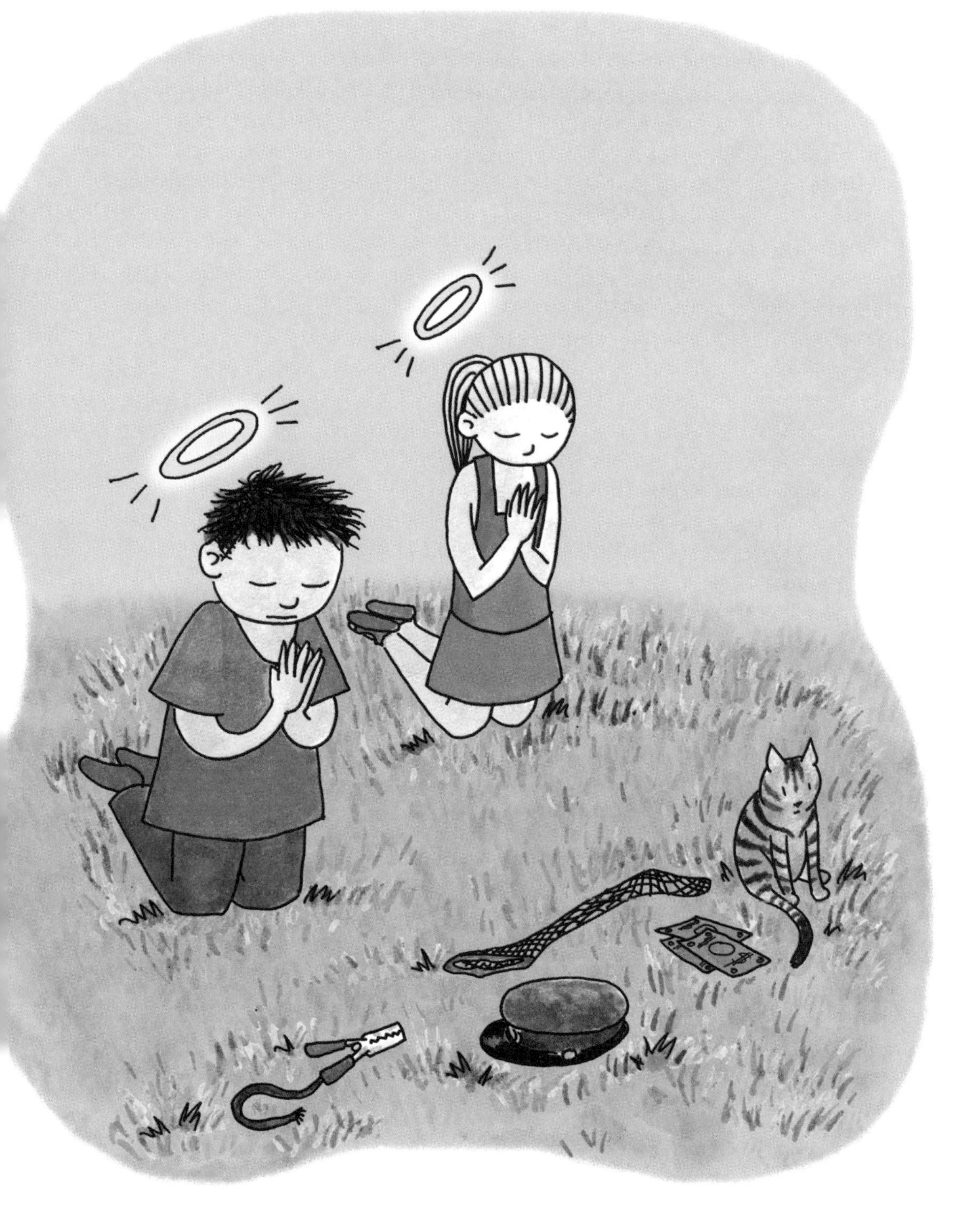

But grandpa wouldn't wake up.

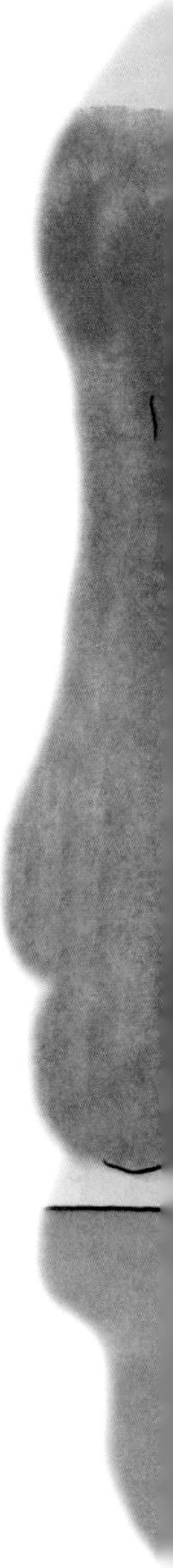

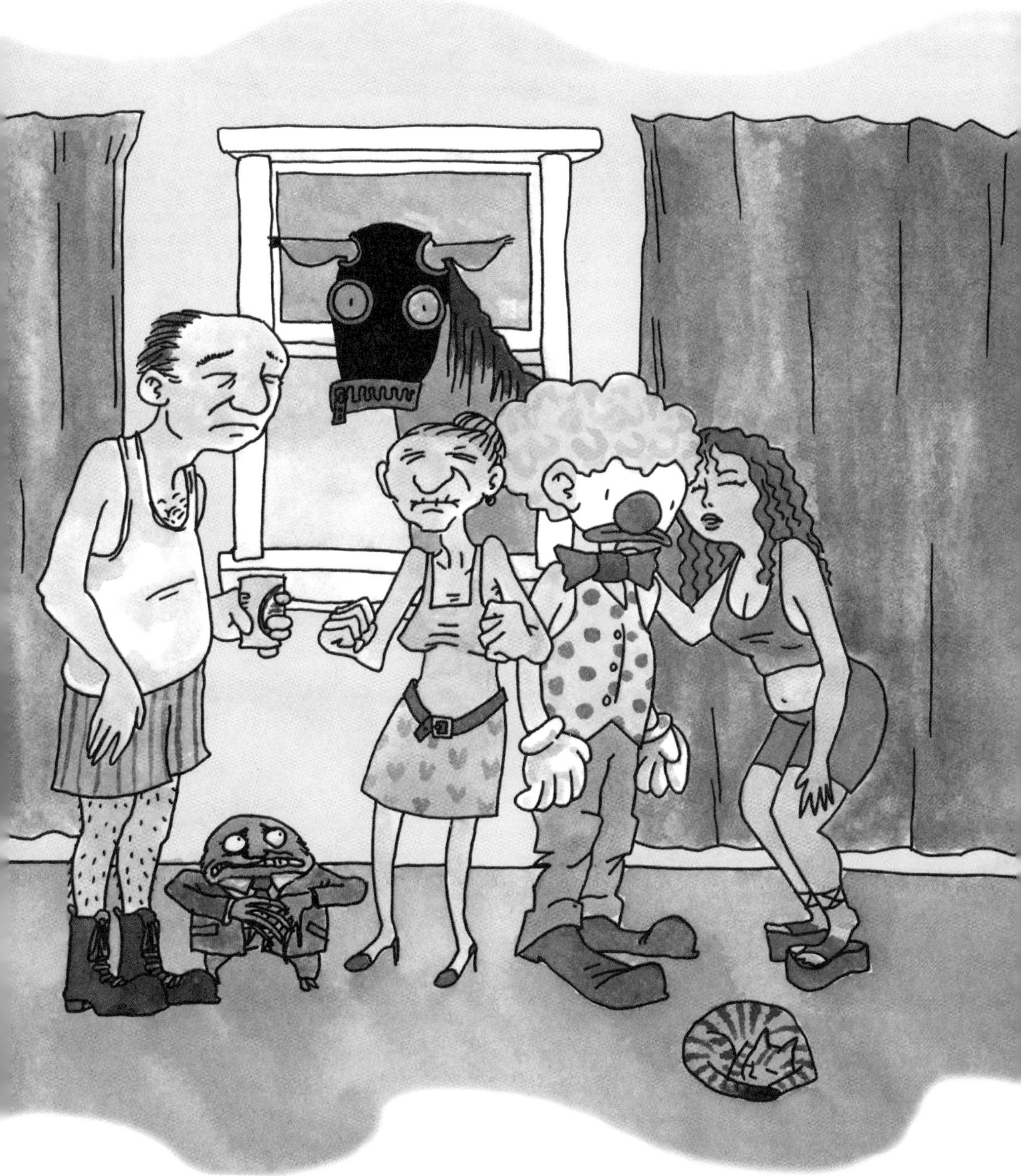

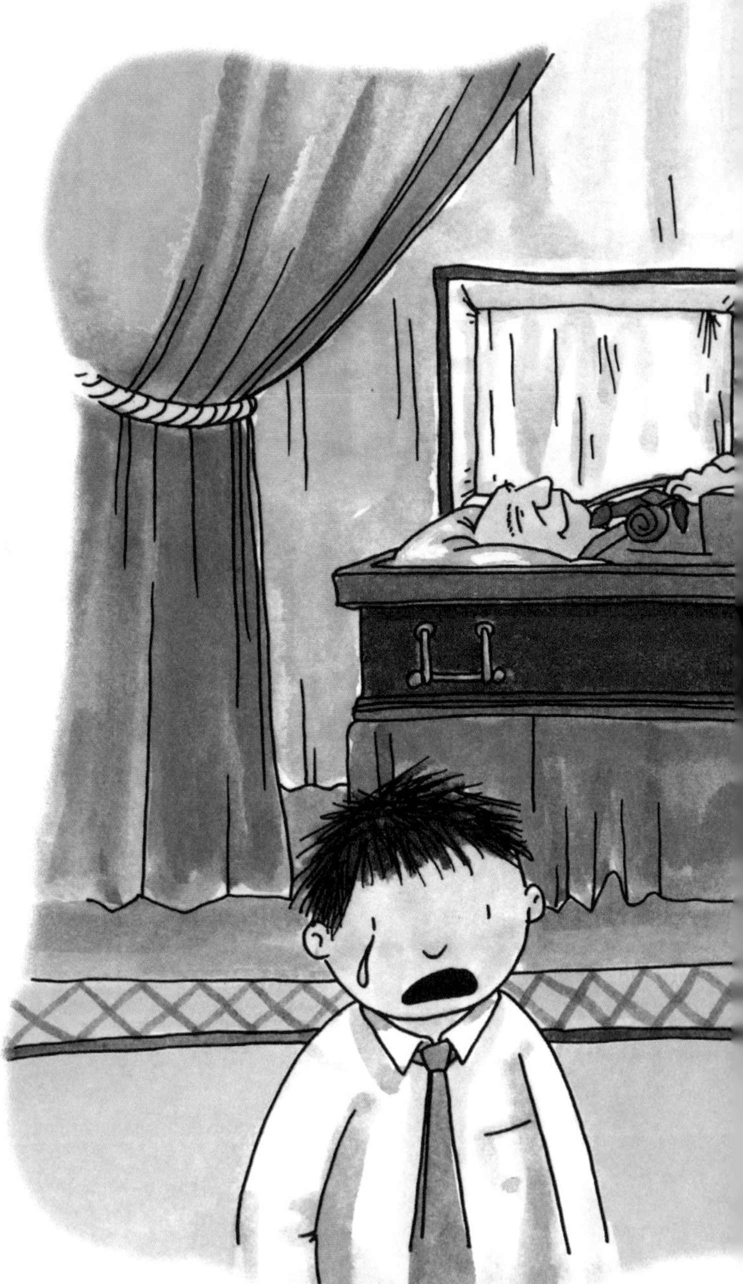

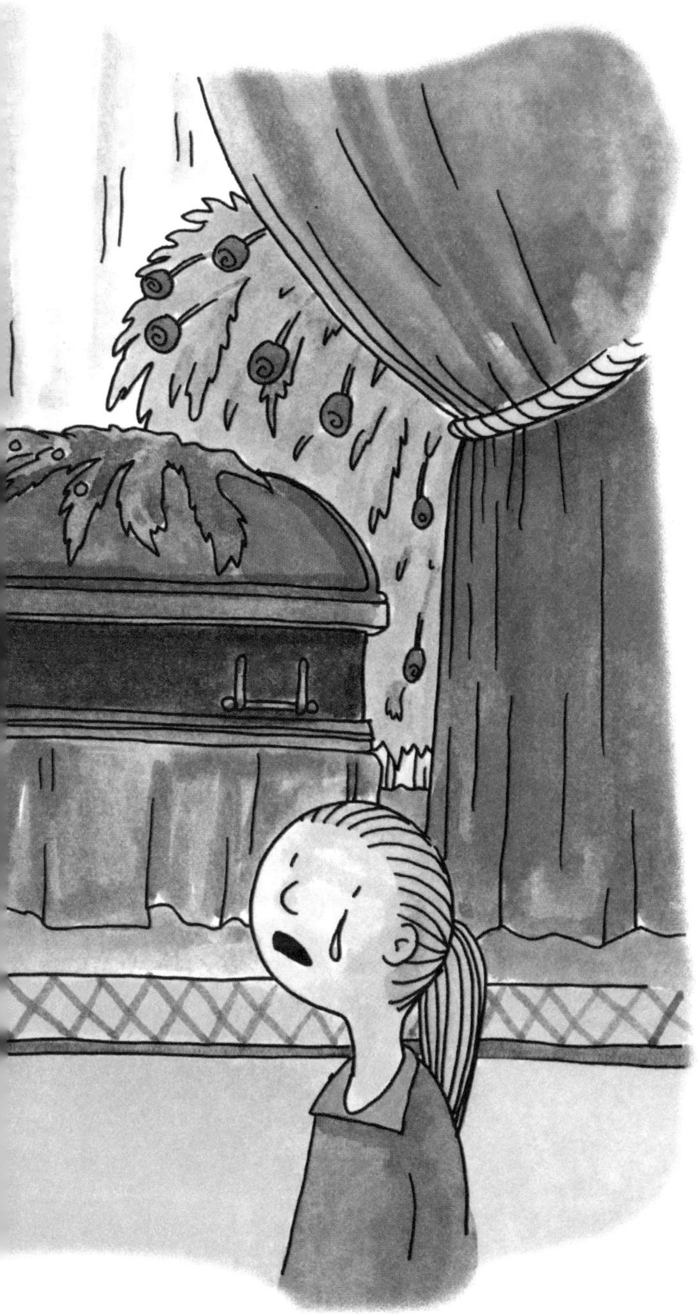

Turns out he was dead.

The End.

simon max hill

simon max hill owns no children, but wrote this thing
for people who keep a children's book on their coffee
table in case of emergency. He also heard from a
reputable source that a urologist would accept a copy
of the book in trade for a vasectomy, and is hoping to
use the money saved there to throw a party to which
you are cordially invited (BYOB). He is unusually
handsome, lives in Portland, and you can find him on
the Internet by searching for
"simon+max+hill+felony+assault."

Shannon Wheeler

Shannon Wheeler has several children, some of which
he considers his own. He lives in Portland, Oregon,
surrounded by animals. *The New Yorker* and *The Onion*
have been known to run his cartoons. He recently won an
award. Sometimes he volunteers at the zoo.

Inquiries about monkey meat can be sent to
www.TMCM.com.

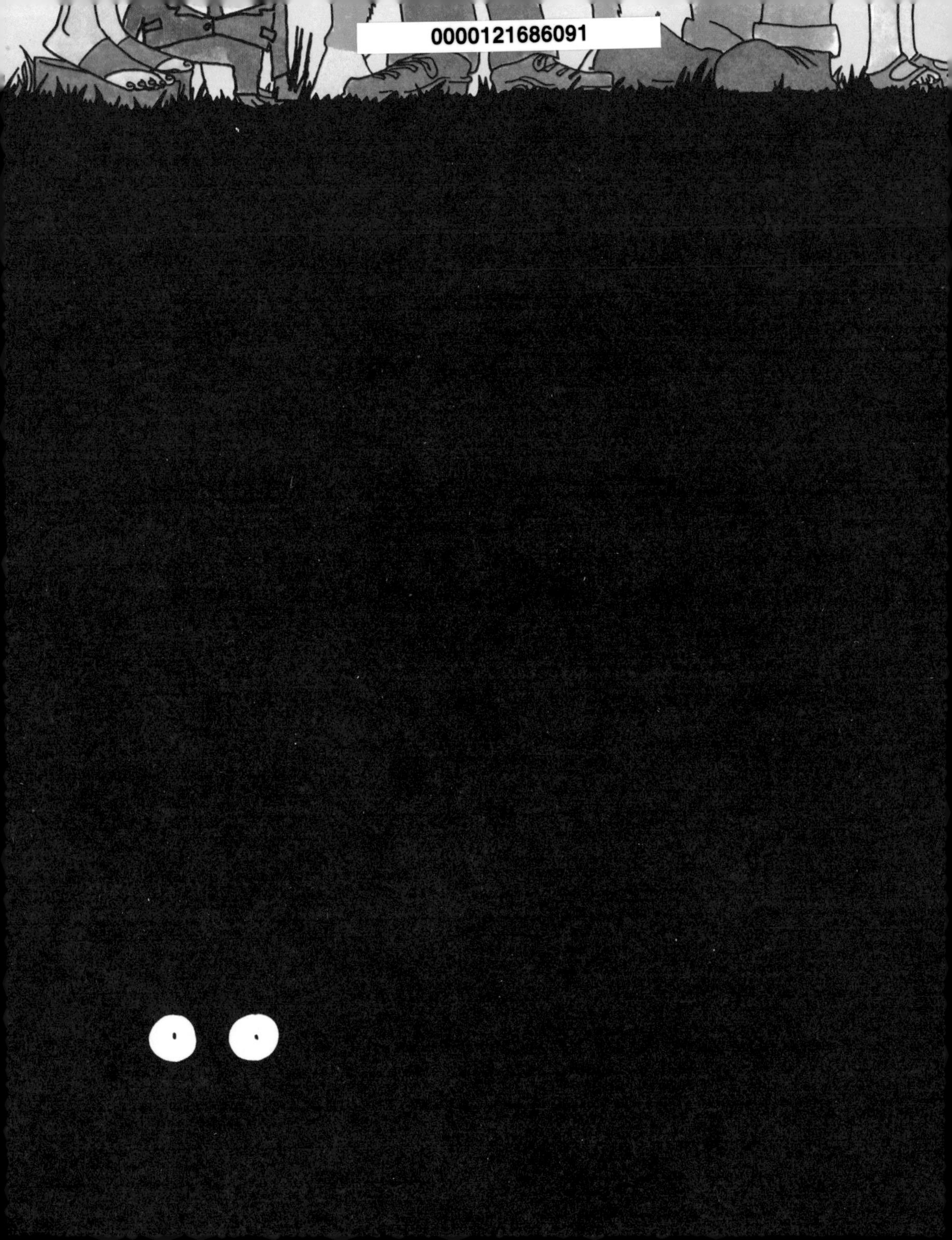